MW01485664

Ann McCallum has learned from God (primarily through the Scriptures) and life (primarily through relationships and ministry). She has learned to be a leader and a follower, a learner and a teacher, a disciple and a spiritual director. Ann takes the pattern that the apostle Paul used in his writing of laying the foundation with Scripture and theology, illustrating it with your own life, and offering some counsel; then she appends some reflection questions and practical ways to make it real in your own life. Those who invest the time and effort to take this journey will certainly benefit.

Dr. Paul Bramer, Professor of Christian Formation and Leadership (retired), Tyndale University, Toronto; Education Director (retired), Emmaus Formation Centre, Mississauga

Ann McCallum is a godly woman, mother, wife, and leader. I have watched and worked with Ann in ministry for many years, when she served as the Executive Director of Highlands Youth for Christ in Orangeville, Ontario. Ann is an authentic woman who leaves health and growth in her path everywhere she goes. Ann is an authentic, real-deal follower of Jesus who has managed her family, run a ministry, and encouraged women around her, all the while faithfully managing life with a non-believing and often challenging husband. For this, Ann has been a hero of mine for many years, someone I dearly look up to. Everything Ann has written in this book is researched, tested, and proven in her own life. She has lived this, and it works.

Tim Coles, National Director, Youth for Christ Canada

To Colin

A great example of
godliness

Ann McCallum

Jan/23

Ann McCallum

A Holy Calling: Becoming a Godly Wife
Copyright ©2022 Ann McCallum
978-1-988928-61-6 Soft Cover
978-1-988928-62-3 E-book

Published by Castle Quay Books
Burlington, Ontario, Canada and Jupiter, Florida, U.S.A.
416-573-3249 | info@castlequaybooks.com | www.castlequaybooks.com

Edited by Marina Hofman Willard
Cover design and book interior by Burst Impressions

Printed in Canada

My heartfelt thanks to Dr. Marina Hofman for her patient and ever-diligent assistance in editing and completing this book, and for the godly women who have walked alongside me throughout my journey, especially my mentor, Sue, and my spiritual director, Birgid.

All rights reserved. This book or parts thereof may not be reproduced in any form without prior written permission of the publishers.

Unless otherwise marked, Scripture quotations are taken from Holy Bible, New International Version® Anglicized, NIV® Copyright © 1979, 1984, 2011 by Biblica, Inc.® Used by permission. All rights reserved worldwide. Scripture quotations marked (NLT) are taken from Holy Bible, New Living Translation, copyright © 1996, 2004, 2015 by Tyndale House Foundation. Used by permission of Tyndale House Publishers, Inc., Carol Stream, Illinois 60188. All rights reserved. Scripture quotations marked (AMP) are taken from the Amplified® Bible, Copyright © 2015 by The Lockman Foundation. Used by permission. www.lockman.org. Scripture quotations marked (MSG) are taken from THE MESSAGE, copyright © 1993, 2002, 2018 by Eugene H. Peterson. Used by permission of NavPress, represented by Tyndale House Publishers. All rights reserved.

Library and Archives Canada Cataloguing in Publication
Title: A holy calling : becoming a Godly wife : a Bible study in 1st Peter / Ann McCallum.
Names: McCallum, Ann, author.
Identifiers: Canadiana 20220150052 | ISBN 9781988928616 (softcover)
Subjects: LCSH: Wives—Prayers and devotions. | LCSH: Marriage—Religious aspects—Christianity. | LCSH: Wives—Religious life. | LCSH: Christian women—Religious life. | LCSH: Bible. Peter, 1st—Criticism, interpretation, etc.
Classification: LCC BV4528.15 .M33 2022 | DDC 248.8/435—dc23

CASTLE QUAY BOOKS

TABLE OF CONTENTS

Part 1

1 PETER
BECOMING

Part 2

FREEDOM FROM UNFORGIVENESS, ANGER, FEAR

FREEDOM THROUGH FORGIVENESS

FREEDOM FROM ANGER

FREEDOM FROM FEAR

Part 3

2 PETER

GROWING

WELCOME TO A JOURNEY

THIS BIBLE STUDY is written for Christian wives, whether your husband is a Christian, backslidden, or non-believing. My husband does not profess faith in Christ, and this is the wilderness where God has kept me living for the past forty years. During that time, my husband made a profession of faith but soon after slipped back into a lifestyle of addictions and a denial of God in his life. When he had an affair and left our family for a time, God opened up the truth of 1 Peter to me, and it changed first my heart and then my way of thinking and behaving toward my husband. When my husband returned home, as difficult as that was, I knew I was different because God had done a marvelous work in my heart. The truths I learned are what I want to share with you now to provide strength for your journey and renewed hope.

Before we begin, please take some time to read 1 Peter straight through. Try to read it through twice before you begin this study. Ask God to open your eyes to His truth for your life and to make your heart receptive to everything He has to say to you.

Let us begin with prayer.

Holy Father in heaven, the One who sees and knows all things, be near to me as I open Your Word. Speak to me through its pages so that my life will be transformed into Your image. Show me, Lord, what resistance I bring, and give me the courage to confess it and let You take it away so that I can become the godly wife that You want me to be to my husband. Keep the interruptions and distractions away from me during this time. I dedicate it to You. Amen.

Each study has an application section to help you work through what the Lord is prompting in your own life. I hope you won't skip this step; you will get a lot more out of the study if you actually take the time to write out your answers and pray through the exercises. God bless you as you spend this time with Him.

Part 1

1 PETER

BECOMING

STUDY #1 OVERVIEW OF 1 PETER

I HAVE READ 1 Peter as many times as I have read through the Bible. I usually read an Old Testament passage, a Gospel passage, and a New Testament passage each day. By passage, I mean either a section under a subheading or a chapter. When I got to 1 Peter 3 and other passages titled "husbands and wives," I used to cringe. I hated reading how Christian husbands were supposed to love their wives and take care of them. I also hated reading that I was supposed to submit to my non-believing husband. I just didn't know how to do that.

It was many years of marriage before I read the whole of 1 Peter in the context of relating to my husband. Actually, it was during a time when I discovered my husband was having an affair that the Lord spoke to me directly about how I needed to be a godly wife to my husband. This truth was paradigm-shifting and changed me forever. It was this truth that I clung to when my husband finally admitted his affair and left my three children and me while he went to live with his mistress. It was this truth that I clung to in hope, knowing that God would return him to us and that this was something God was using to bring my husband to Himself.

APPLICATION

What stands out to you as you read through 1 Peter?

How has God specifically spoken to you?

What surprised you?

What unsettled you?

What challenged you?

Begin a journal of your journey through 1 Peter where you can share your thoughts and prayers with the Lord. Writing down what you process before God will help cement it in your thinking and provide a record for you when you need to be reminded in the future. Make sure it's kept where no one else will find it, so that you can be completely honest. I also suggest you find another strong Christian woman you can trust, and ask her to pray with you as you go through this study—someone you know will keep your confidence and who will not be afraid to speak truthfully to you when you need it. I recommend meeting with this woman weekly for prayer, even if it's over the phone. Read through 1 Peter once more, this time in the context of how you are to be a godly wife. Not just chapter 3, but the whole book.

May God bless you as you embark on this journey.

#2 SPIRITUAL WARFARE

Ephesians 6:10–18:

[10] Finally, be strong in the Lord and in his mighty power. [11] Put on the full armour of God, so that you can take your stand against the devil's schemes. [12] For our struggle is not against flesh and blood, but against the rulers, against the authorities, against the powers of this dark world and against the spiritual forces of evil in the heavenly realms. [13] Therefore put on the full armour of God, so that when the day of evil comes, you may be able to stand your ground, and after you have done everything, to stand. [14] Stand firm then, with the belt of truth buckled round your waist, with the breastplate of righteousness in place, [15] and with your feet fitted with the readiness that comes from the gospel of peace. [16] In addition to all this, take up the shield of faith, with which you can extinguish all the flaming arrows of the evil one. [17] Take the helmet of salvation and the sword of the Spirit, which is the word of God.

[18] And pray in the Spirit on all occasions with all kinds of prayers and requests. With this in mind, be alert and always keep on praying for all the Lord's people.

IF YOU REALLY want to seek the Lord's will for your life and for your marriage, then the enemy of our souls, Satan, is not going to like it. Although I am not the type who sees "a demon around every corner," I do believe it is wise to be aware of his tactics and prepare for them. He knows what buttons to push, so decide in advance how you're going to respond differently. The attack may not come directly through your husband; it could be finances, health, family, or a host of other things that the enemy uses to distract you. Decide now to resolutely follow the Lord and do His will, and persevere through this study and your pursuit of being a godly wife.

Remember that God told us to expect opposition and gave us armour to defend ourselves. Read Ephesians 6:10–18, and ask the Lord to equip you. Be aware of the enemy's schemes, and pray regularly for protection. When worry, doubt, or fear assails you, cling to the Lord and His promise that He will never leave you or forsake you.

Your journey toward becoming a godly wife is God's will for you. There will be times you are tempted to quit, get out, or fight back. If you fall, call on the Lord for forgiveness, and get right back on the path. If you are not tempted, and if you are not receiving some type of opposition, then it's very likely you are not following the Lord. It just comes with the territory.

Find a verse of Scripture that speaks to your situation specifically. It could be Philippians 4:6, 8, 13, or 19. It could be Isaiah 40:31 or 41:10. Whatever it is, memorize it, and carry it around with you in your heart. Or write it on a sticky note and put it somewhere you will always see it, like your computer or the dashboard of your car. Hold on to the truth of God and by doing so defeat the lies of the enemy.

Proverbs 3:5–6: "Trust in the LORD with all your heart and lean not on your own understanding; in all your ways submit to him, and he will make your paths straight."

APPLICATION

What decisions do you need to make in order to persevere through this study and your pursuit of being a godly wife? It may help you to set a time and location to meet with the Lord daily. A "time" doesn't need to be exactly the same hour on the clock each day, but part of your routine. (For example, I get up, shower, pour a coffee, and sit down with my Bible first thing each day whether it's at 5, 6, or 7 a.m.) Commit this in writing to the Lord.

Read Ephesians 6: 10–18 and ask the Lord to equip you. You may find it helpful to visualize putting on the armour every day. Are there other pieces of self-made armour you need to take off, like deception, in order to put on the belt of truth?

Find a verse or section of Scripture to journey with you, write it out and make sure it's visible to you multiple times a day until you memorize it.

#3 PLANKEYE

Matthew 7:1–5:
[1] "Do not judge, or you too will be judged. [2] For in the same way as you judge others, you will be judged, and with the measure you use, it will be measured to you.

[3] "Why do you look at the speck of sawdust in your brother's eye and pay no attention to the plank in your own eye? [4] How can you say to your brother, 'Let me take the speck out of your eye,' when all the time there is a plank in your own eye? [5] You hypocrite, first take the plank out of your own eye, and then you will see clearly to remove the speck from your brother's eye."

SOMETIMES I GET really irritated with my husband. I see the same behaviours over and over, and it never changes. Actually, that's not true; it gets worse. I spend countless hours begging God to change my situation and to change him. It's very disheartening to see how much time has passed and there hasn't been any improvement; no movement toward the Lord; no ownership of the issues and the damage they are causing our family; no indication that he even realizes or cares. I want to cry along with the psalmist, day after day, "How long, O Lord? Will You forget me forever?"

The one thing I have learned after thirty-six long years of pleading with God is that He is going to work in *my* life and in my heart before He answers these prayers. Not that God isn't working in my husband's life too; but God is far more interested in talking to me about myself and my issues. I have discovered that there's a spiritual principle at work, outlined in Matthew 7:1–5, that has never failed in any of my relationships and is first and foremost in my marriage: "In the same way you judge others, you will be judged, and with the measure you use, it will be measured to you." The very same things that are annoying you about the other person are evident in *your* life.

God wants you to see how you are behaving toward Him. It is only as you recognize, acknowledge, confess, and repent of your sin that God will help you deal with the other person—which may be just an attitude adjustment in you and not a total makeover of your husband. We are quick to see the speck in our husband's life, and in the meantime, we are carrying around a plank of the same sin in our own lives.

We forget sometimes that God helps us remove that plank in our eye so that we can help our brother (or husband) remove the speck from his eye. Which is more difficult to remove, the plank or the speck? As I said, this is somewhere God has always taken me when I am well caught up in how I've got to deal with another person. Try it; it doesn't fail. On the surface, you may not think you have anything like your husband's sin in your life but God wants you to hear: you do.

APPLICATION

Think of something that's really bothering you that your husband is doing. Make a list of why that is bothering you: how it affects you, how he acts when he's like that, and the collateral damage he's causing you.

Quiet yourself before the Lord, and ask the Holy Spirit to bring to mind the ways you're being like this. Write down what the Holy Spirit impresses on your heart and mind.

Acknowledge and confess your sin before God, don't leave it undealt with. Write out your prayer.

Repent: this involves a turning, a change of direction. What do you need to do instead?

How will you do that?

How will you keep from falling back into the sin God has shown you? Again, make lists.

Put it into action! Once you have taken stock of your own life, prayerfully ask God if there's anything you need to do to help your husband. It is my experience that the answer always comes easily at this point. However, it's not always an action or something I need to say; often it's a renewal of trust in God or a change of attitude (usually humility) on my part.

#4 THE TRUTH ABOUT YOU

1 Peter 1:1–2:
¹ Peter, an apostle of Jesus Christ,

To God's elect, exiles, scattered throughout the provinces of Pontus, Galatia, Cappadocia, Asia and Bithynia, ² who have been chosen according to the foreknowledge of God the Father, through the sanctifying work of the Spirit, to be obedient to Jesus Christ and sprinkled with his blood:

Grace and peace be yours in abundance.

SINCE I'VE ALREADY had you take a strong look at sin and negative things in your life, let's go to 1 Peter 1 and take a look at some positive things. It's easy to believe lies about yourself, especially if you have someone's voice in your ear or in your head telling you that everything's your fault, that you're stupid, that you're worthless, or something equally as bad. God wants you to hear the truth: that's not how you are at all.

First Peter is written to God's elect—those who are His children and who believe in Him and follow His Son, Jesus Christ. Is that you? Have you accepted God's gift of salvation, freely given by His grace through Jesus's sacrifice and death on the cross? Have you been given new life through the resurrection of Jesus? If so, then you are a new creation (see 2 Corinthians 5:17). You are one of the elect that Peter is writing to. You are chosen according to God's foreknowledge of you, your life, and your situation. Chosen for sanctifying, that is, to be set apart and made holy so that you can be obedient to Jesus Christ. Nothing about you is an accident. God picked you out to be special; to be His own, and to have a purpose.

To know God is sanctifying you is important. God is at work shaping you into the person He has designed you to be, and sometimes you won't like the instruments He has selected for that process. Think of a craftsman smoothing a fine piece of wood by rubbing it with sandpaper over and over. What sandpaper has God chosen to smooth out your rough edges? Do you object to His tools as He pokes you, as He tries to show you things in your life that you'd rather ignore? This is all His effort in sanctification. Praise God, that He loves you as you are, but He loves you too much to leave you that way. Don't fight Him as He shapes you into a beautiful masterpiece. Remember that He is your loving creator, and He is still creating you.

APPLICATION

How does it make you feel to know you are chosen by God?

To explore this further, read Ephesians 1:3–14, and write down all the wonderful promises God has given you.

Ephesians 1:3–14:

3 Praise be to the God and Father of our Lord Jesus Christ, who has blessed us in the heavenly realms with every spiritual blessing in Christ. 4 For he chose us in him before the creation of the world to be holy and blameless in his sight. In love 5 he predestined us for adoption to sonship through Jesus Christ, in accordance with his pleasure and will—6 to the praise of his glorious grace, which he has freely given us in the One he loves. 7 In him we have redemption through his blood, the forgiveness of sins, in accordance with the riches of God's grace 8 that he lavished on us. With all wisdom and understanding, 9 he made known to us the mystery of his will according to his good pleasure, which he purposed in Christ, 10 to be put into effect when the times reach their fulfillment—to bring unity to all things in heaven and on earth under Christ.

11 In him we were also chosen, having been predestined according to the plan of him who works out everything in conformity with the purpose of his will, 12 in order that we, who were the first to put our hope in Christ, might be for the

praise of his glory. [13] And you also were included in Christ when you heard the message of truth, the gospel of your salvation. When you believed, you were marked in him with a seal, the promised Holy Spirit, [14] who is a deposit guaranteeing our inheritance until the redemption of those who are God's possession—to the praise of his glory.

What instruments has God been using to sanctify you and make you into His beautiful masterpiece?

Talk with God about how you're feeling. You may need to ask forgiveness for ways you've been resisting His work of chiseling your life. Praise Him for all that He's doing, even those things you may not like very much. Write them down, and ask Him for special grace in those areas where it is especially difficult.

#5 LIVING HOPE

1 Peter 1:3–5:

3 Praise be to the God and Father of our Lord Jesus Christ! In his great mercy he has given us new birth into a living hope through the resurrection of Jesus Christ from the dead, 4 and into an inheritance that can never perish, spoil or fade. This inheritance is kept in heaven for you, 5 who through faith are shielded by God's power until the coming of the salvation that is ready to be revealed in the last time.

IS YOUR HOPE dead or alive? Test yourself by asking these questions: Do I expect nothing but bad to happen? Do I really expect God to change my current situation? When I picture the future, do I imagine it with my marriage and my life better, or the same, or worse? Am I asking God to work things out, yet in the back of my mind figuring out my Plan B if He doesn't? Have I resigned myself to the belief that nothing will change for the good and planned accordingly?

I could keep going, but I think you get the idea. Most of us long ago gave up on things actually working out for our good. Is that you? Do you want God's will, or are you not sure you do anymore? Have you lost hope? I was jarred at the discovery of this in my life when I read Matthew 13:58: "He did not do many miracles there because of their lack of faith." Has my unbelief kept God from working? Has yours?

First Peter 1:3 says, "He has given us new birth into a living hope." What would it look like to have a hope that's alive? The Amplified Version renders verse 3 this way: "who according to His abundant and boundless mercy has caused us to be born again [that is, to be re-born from above—spiritually transformed, renewed, and set apart for His purpose] to an ever-living hope and confident assurance through the resurrection of Jesus Christ from the dead." Let the truth of this statement sink in for a few moments. *You.* Transformed. Renewed. Set apart for His purpose. Ever-living hope. Confident assurance. Not because you have done or do anything, but because Jesus rose from the dead and is now living. Spend some time thinking about each one of those words and letting it wash over you. Journal how your life can change if you live as though you believe it.

In verses 4 and 5 we read, "[born anew] into an inheritance which is imperishable [beyond the reach of change] and undefiled and unfading, reserved in heaven for you, who are being protected *and* shielded by the power of God through your faith for salvation" (AMP). What do you understand this inheritance to be? Have you ever had anyone leave you an inheritance? Suppose you had an extremely wealthy relative who loved you thoroughly, and that person told you they were leaving you an inheritance. If the possibility of an earthly inheritance brings that much anticipation, our heavenly inheritance should be that much more! No matter what happens to us in this life, you can be sure that you have an inheritance that is reserved for you. God's promises do not fail, and He does not lie. Allow yourself to soak in this truth for a few moments.

APPLICATION

Is your hope dead or alive? Test yourself by asking these questions: Do I expect nothing but bad to happen?

Do I really expect God to change my current situation?

When I picture the future, do I imagine it with my marriage and my life better, or the same, or worse?

Am I asking God to work things out, yet in the back of my mind figuring out my Plan B if He doesn't?

Have I resigned myself to the belief that nothing will change for the good and planned accordingly?

Ask God to forgive you of negative thoughts and to reshape your thinking.

Take some time now to thank God for the things you have learned from this passage. Write a poem, letter, song, or thank-you note to God for His love, mercy, and grace toward you. Spend some time talking with Him about how much you long to be with Him. Use your imagination to walk alongside Him as He tells you the exciting things He has planned for you. Be blessed.

#6 FOR A LITTLE WHILE

1 Peter 1:6–12:

⁶ In all this you greatly rejoice, though now for a little while you may have had to suffer grief in all kinds of trials. ⁷ These have come so that the proven genuineness of your faith—of greater worth than gold, which perishes even though refined by fire—may result in praise, glory and honour when Jesus Christ is revealed. ⁸ Though you have not seen him, you love him; and even though you do not see him now, you believe in him and are filled with an inexpressible and glorious joy, ⁹ for you are receiving the end result of your faith, the salvation of your souls.

¹⁰ Concerning this salvation, the prophets, who spoke of the grace that was to come to you, searched intently and with the greatest care, ¹¹ trying to find out the time and circumstances to which the Spirit of Christ in them was pointing when he predicted the sufferings of the Messiah and the glories that would follow. ¹² It was revealed to them that they were not serving themselves but you, when they spoke of the things that have now been told you by those who have preached the gospel to you by the Holy Spirit sent from heaven. Even angels long to look into these things.

AFTER SPENDING TIME dwelling on living hope, I think you can agree with Peter that "in all this you greatly rejoice." It's good to keep an eternal perspective and learn to focus there when we have bad days. As he says, "though now for a little while you may have had to suffer grief in all kinds of trials."

Take that apart for a minute:

"Now": These are your current trials. They are not your whole past life, although sometimes it feels like that. They are not your future, although sometimes we live like they will be. They are now, and they will pass.

"For a little while": They are not forever; they are not even for a long time. Do you act like your troubles are your second skin, your tattoo that brands you for the rest of your life? They aren't. From

God's perspective, this is merely a blip in time, like a henna tattoo that will wash off in a few days. Don't act as if it's a life sentence.

"You may have had to suffer grief": Read that again. You *may* have had to. It doesn't mean you will. It doesn't mean you will continue to. These trials are only what God deems necessary; they are only for a purpose, and they don't happen to everyone. Although someone else has been through a trial, that doesn't mean it will happen to you. Don't fixate on someone else's outcome of a similar situation. God does not work in everyone's life the same way. Put your eyes on Him.

"In all kinds of trials": Not everyone's struggles are the same, and God brings the tools to chisel you that He knows will help you most. He's developing you into a unique masterpiece, not copying His work in someone else's life. There are many ways you may struggle; and He knows what you can take that someone else cannot. Suffering doesn't wear only one face; it has many different faces.

The purpose? "These have come so that the ... genuineness of your faith—of greater worth than gold, which perishes even though refined by fire" may be proven. God is proving your faith through testing, and He is moulding and shaping you so that your new creation will be even more beautiful. Your faith is precious—more valuable than gold. But it needs refining, just as gold does. It will become even more precious, so even the refining is valuable. How awesome our amazing God is, to take such an interest in you and your faith.

The result? "The proven genuineness of your faith ... may result in praise, glory and honour when Jesus Christ is revealed." Once your faith is proven genuine, it will result in praise, glory, and honour to Jesus. Think through the ways this may occur, your life bringing glory and honour to Him. There is joy in anticipation of this goal. "Though you have not seen him, you love him; and even though you do not see him now, you believe in him and are filled with an *inexpressible and glorious joy,* for you are receiving the goal of your faith, the salvation of your souls" (emphasis added). Ask the Lord to fill you with this joy.

APPLICATION

Read Romans 5:3-5 and James 1:2-4. Write down all the glorious outcomes of your faith-refining suffering. Personalize it to your own life.

Romans 5:3-5: "Not only so, but we also glory in our sufferings, because we know that suffering produces perseverance; perseverance, character; and character, hope. And hope does not put us to shame, because God's love has been poured out into our hearts through the Holy Spirit, who has been given to us."

James 1:2-4: "Consider it pure joy, my brothers and sisters, whenever you face trials of many kinds, because you know that the testing of your faith produces perseverance. Let perseverance finish its work so that you may be mature and complete, not lacking anything."

Think of your life bringing glory and honour to God. How is that different from the life you live now?

In what ways do you want to change that? Ask Him to reveal to you next steps.

Do you long for inexpressible and glorious joy? Sit quietly with the Lord, and tell Him how much you love Him. Ask Him to give you this gift.

#7 SO WHAT AM I SUPPOSED TO DO NOW?

1 Peter 1:13–16:
¹³ Therefore, with minds that are alert and fully sober, set your hope on the grace to be brought to you when Jesus Christ is revealed at his coming. ¹⁴ As obedient children, do not conform to the evil desires you had when you lived in ignorance. ¹⁵ But just as he who called you is holy, so be holy in all you do; ¹⁶ for it is written: "Be holy, because I am holy."

FIRST PETER 1:13 indicates that you should "prepare your minds for action" (NLT). You are to get mentally ready for what God is going to do in your life and what you are going to do to adjust. It is coming, and He is asking you to *prepare*. Once I thought I was prepared (or at least, preparing); but when I read these words, I examined my life, what I had been doing, and how I had been viewing myself and my future. I had a revelation: Now I'm just lazy. No action came, or it passed me by. Or maybe the truth is that I ignored it. I thought of Moses and the burning bush (see Exodus 3); what if he had seen it and just kept on walking by? I was suspicious I had been doing that in my life.

Verse 13 continues: "Exercise self-control" (NLT). I blew that too. "Set your hope on the grace to be brought to you." Hope. It's in the Lord. I thought, *What have I done but mess it all up? I'm unprepared. I lack even the measure of self-control I once had.* But I am not hopeless, despite how I feel. And neither are you.

Does your heart cry out, "Change me, Lord"?—the way He changed Paul (see Acts 9) and Gideon (see Judges 6–7), who I relate to when I feel like yelling, "Who am I? The least of the least." Just as the disciples protested when Jesus asked them to feed the 5,000 (see Luke 9:13), I asked, "You expect me to what?" All these references are about God calling people who did not expect or deserve the honour—people who were unworthy, insignificant, sinful, or hiding. Tired and ill-equipped. Just like me.

First Peter says, "Prepare your minds for action," "be self-controlled," and "be holy"; yet I have been ignoring God. I want to roll these all in a ball and say, "But I'm the least and the weakest! I'm a scoundrel who has been fighting God, and my hands are dirty! I have nothing to give physically or emotionally—and besides, I thought Jesus said, 'Come away and rest.'" But just as in Luke 9, the boat has landed, rest time is over, and my store of "food" is meager. And now God is asking me to do impossible things.

God is telling you it's time for action, and you should be excited, getting ready. Prepare your mind for *action*. Be self-controlled. Set your hope fully on the grace to be *given* you. It's time to be an *obedient* child of God. Start behaving like one. *Do not conform* to the evil desires you had when you lived in ignorance of your calling as a wife, your purpose, your deeper faith. Once you've realized this truth and you know it, you can no longer pretend you don't. Just as He is holy, *so be holy* in all you do.

APPLICATION

Do you wonder what to do now? Listen for the still small voice. Perhaps you sense the Holy Spirit saying, "Do what's in front of you."

What else has He been saying? *Prepare.* God has a plan; have you been preparing for action, or have you been preparing for inaction? Are you taking the easy route and just letting things happen to you, choosing to do nothing?

What have you been prepping your mind for?

Self-control means saying no to impulses. Dallas Willard has a brilliant description of temptation in *Renovation of the Heart*: "Sin itself is when we inwardly say 'yes' to the temptation, when we *would* do the deed, even though we may not actually get to carry it out."[1] In what areas do you lack self-control?

How can you prepare for more self-control?

Personalize this phrase: "Set my hope fully on the grace to be given me." What is your hope set on?

What does it look like for you to hope for grace?

How can you set your hope on grace to be given you "in the moment" of your conflict? Watch for Jesus to reveal Himself.

---

1. Dallas Willard and Jan Johnson, *Renovation of the Heart in Daily Practice: Experiments in Spiritual Transformation* (Carol Stream: Tyndale House, 2006), 27.

Grace (getting what you don't deserve): What does that look like in your marriage?

How has God provided grace to your husband through you?

#8 SELF CONTROL

1 Peter 1:13–16:

¹³ Therefore, with minds that are alert and fully sober, set your hope on the grace to be brought to you when Jesus Christ is revealed at his coming. ¹⁴ As obedient children, do not conform to the evil desires you had when you lived in ignorance. ¹⁵ But just as he who called you is holy, so be holy in all you do; ¹⁶ for it is written: "Be holy, because I am holy."

"SO PREPARE YOUR minds for action and exercise self-control" (1 Peter 1:13 NLT). We all have some measure of self-control. When your husband infuriates you, you don't scream, throw up your hands, and walk away. You don't punch people when they make you angry. You walk past the freezer rather than grabbing the ice cream every time you feel like it.

But you will also agree that most of us don't have the level of self-control we would like to have. We may be right in thinking we have more than the next person, but we know that God doesn't give out gold stars, and He's not comparing us with the next person. He is comparing us with His standard, and "be self-controlled" is a command. Therefore, lacking self-control is sinful.

Again I refer to Dallas Willard's *Renovation of the Heart*, which speaks of the body responses that "take over," controlled by the flesh and not the Spirit. Like not looking at people when they speak to you, interrupting them (out loud and in your head), looking around when someone is talking, pacing or wagging your finger when you get wound up. When it's someone you dislike or discredit, you may find you shut down when they speak. Or you let your mind wander. What we all need is to retrain our bodies to listen and to silence our own thoughts. If you're like me, you put your own thoughts before others, thinking your own thoughts are more important. Lord, forgive us. This is sin.

How do we retrain? Try praying before every conversation, whether it's live or by phone or electronically. Pray before you answer the phone or open an email. Listen for the Holy Spirit's whispers and pay attention. Settle and silence yourself first; listen to what the other person is saying; pray again; silence yourself again; listen for the Lord and *then* speak. When talking to another person, think, *I'm going to focus on you; you are important, and I really want to hear what you have to say.* Ask the Lord for wisdom, and expect Him to answer, because He has promised He will (James 1:5).

APPLICATION

"Prepare your mind for action" has the idea of gathering up your skirts to run. Ask the Lord how to do that mentally. What are your next steps?

What inner qualities exist in the various aspects of yourself, and what do they dictate to your body?

What are some action steps you can take to retrain? Go through the next one or two days and watch for areas where you need retraining for better self-control. Ask the Holy Spirit to remind you and to guide you as you seek to strengthen your self-control.

Review and write down the action steps listed above. Practice praying before every conversation in this way. Journal the changes that you see in your life and conversations. "May thy dear Son preserve me from this present evil world, so that its smiles never allure, nor its frowns terrify, nor its vices defile, nor its errors delude me."[2]

---

2. *The Valley of Vision: A Collection of Puritan Prayers and Devotions*, ed. Arthur Bennett (East Peoria: Versa Press, 2015), 44.

#9 CONFORMING?

1 Peter 1:13–22:

¹³ Therefore, with minds that are alert and fully sober, set your hope on the grace to be brought to you when Jesus Christ is revealed at his coming. ¹⁴ As obedient children, do not conform to the evil desires you had when you lived in ignorance. ¹⁵ But just as he who called you is holy, so be holy in all you do; ¹⁶ for it is written: "Be holy, because I am holy."

¹⁷ Since you call on a Father who judges each person's work impartially, live out your time as foreigners here in reverent fear. ¹⁸ For you know that it was not with perishable things such as silver or gold that you were redeemed from the empty way of life handed down to you from your ancestors, ¹⁹ but with the precious blood of Christ, a lamb without blemish or defect. ²⁰ He was chosen before the creation of the world, but was revealed in these last times for your sake. ²¹ Through him you believe in God, who raised him from the dead and glorified him, and so your faith and hope are in God.

²² Now that you have purified yourselves by obeying the truth so that you have sincere love for each other, love one another deeply, from the heart.

WE ARE STILL pondering the "be prepared" command from 1 Peter 1:13 and how to flesh that out. For a long time, I knew the Lord was telling me to wait and rest. But now He's giving me action words. Ask the Lord to open your eyes and ears to what He may be saying to you.

First Peter 1 teaches you how to be prepared. Notice my emphasis in verse 14: "As obedient children, *do not conform* to the evil desires you had when you lived in ignorance." *Valley of Vision* states, "May I ... *conform* to Him as my example" (emphasis added).³ Ask the Lord Jesus to help you conform to Him. To be holy.

I usually know what *not* to conform to, but what *do* I conform to? His way. As it says in verse 22, you "purify yourself by obeying the truth" and "have sincere love for each other." "Love one another

---

3. *The Valley of Vision*, 44.

deeply, from the heart." Do you? Or do you need to pray, "Lord, my heart doesn't love real deeply, so You'll need to work"?

But that's what pursuing Christlikeness is about, right? So much of self-control and retraining are tied together. Although you have pegged lots of wrong autoresponses, are there more? How about facial expressions, rolling eyes, stiffening of back and jaw, flaring nostrils, sneering behind another's back? All of these have *self* and *pride* at the root. Ask the Lord to chop down this tree at the root, rework your inner core, and show you how to cooperate with His work in you.

APPLICATION

If the Lord is bringing you out of a time of *wait and rest*, what action words is He giving you? Ask the Lord to open your eyes and ears to what He may be saying to you. Ask the Lord Jesus to help you conform to Him. To be holy.

What are things you should not conform to but find yourself tempted?

What specific ways should you conform to Christ's example to counter these?

What are next steps for you to do that?

"Love one another deeply, from the heart." Do you?

Pray, "Lord, my heart doesn't love real deeply, so You'll need to work. Show me how to love *without hypocrisy*." Ask the Lord to reveal a deeper level of self and pride that is showing through in your facial features, tone of voice, go-to phrases. Ask Him to give you actions or words to replace these.

#10 BECOMING CHRISTLIKE

1 Peter 1:22–25:
²² Now that you have purified yourselves by obeying the truth so that you have sincere love for each other, love one another deeply, from the heart. ²³ For you have been born again, not of perishable seed, but of imperishable, through the living and enduring word of God. ²⁴ For,
    "All people are like grass,
    and all their glory is like the flowers of the field;
    the grass withers and the flowers fall,
    ²⁵ but the word of the Lord endures forever."
    And this is the word that was preached to you.

DO YOU BELIEVE it's possible to be Christlike? It must be, if God expects it of us. There's no point in trying to move forward if we really don't believe anything will change. But we have been "born again, not of perishable seed, but of imperishable" (1 Peter 1:23). Think about what imperishable means. Does not die. Cannot fail. Born from above and set apart for a purpose, "through the living and enduring word of God." He said it, so you can trust it.

When you read verse 24, what comes to mind? If all people are like grass, what qualities does that imply? If "all their glory is like the flowers of the field," what does that mean for the future? "The grass withers and the flowers fall." It's gone in a breath of wind.

I hear a lot these days about envisioning one's *preferred future*. The problem is, when you get a picture of your preferred future in your head, you can grab it tightly in your hands and try to control it, try to make it happen. Up to a point, that's a good thing; but if your vision is not the same as God's vision of your future, you may as well be holding cut flowers in your hands and willing them to live. They won't. Even the most beautiful flowers will eventually die and blooms fall. Human glory is like that. And it looks pretty ugly when it's dying too.

God's future plans for you aren't like that. When He calls you to Christlikeness, it's a sure thing. It is more like the Israelites being told to go up and possess the land (see Joshua 1:11). God promised it, He gave it to them, and it was theirs, but they had to do the work to take it. It still had to be conquered; the enemies needed to be driven out, and they needed to physically start their new life in that place. It takes time, it takes planning, and it takes action. God gives us the grace for all of this. Second Corinthians 9:8 states, "God is able to bless you abundantly, so that in all things at all times, having all that you need, you will abound in every good work."

What promised land is God showing you? Becoming like Christ, becoming a godly wife, acting and reacting righteously toward your husband! Do you believe transformation can happen?

The word of the Lord endures forever. What is His word to you today?

APPLICATION

How would your marriage change if you were more Christlike? Confess to the Lord the areas where you are lacking, and ask Him to do a work of transformation in your heart.

In what ways is your life like withering grass?

What are the *cut flowers* in your life that you are holding on to so tightly that are withering as time goes on?

What does God want to replace the *cut flowers* of your preferred future with?

What promised land is God showing you?

Write down what you're sure about (Christlikeness, being a godly wife), and ask God to show you what else He envisions.

"But the word of the Lord endures forever." What is His word to you today?

#11 FIRST THINGS FIRST

1 Peter 2:1–3:
¹ Therefore, rid yourselves of all malice and all deceit, hypocrisy, envy, and slander of every kind. ² Like newborn babies, crave pure spiritual milk, so that by it you may grow up in your salvation, ³ now that you have tasted that the Lord is good.

TO CONFORM TO the image of Christ, 1 Peter 2 tells us there are things we have to get rid of in our lives. You may have already identified those in our previous study. Again, this requires preparation and action on your part. There is a list in 1 Peter 2:1 of things you must "rid yourself" of: all malice and deceit, hypocrisy, envy, and slander of every kind. Are those things at work in your life? Since we are focusing on marriage, start by examining how they are evident in your relationship with your husband.

Notice it says *all* malice. Do you have malicious thoughts? Do you think things you would never dare say out loud? Do you ever secretly hope something will happen to your husband to teach him a lesson? All kinds of malice must go.

How about deceit? Ever keep secrets or tell partial truths or hide things or information from your husband?

Hypocrisy is the practice of saying one thing and doing another. Do you have different standards for your husband that you don't uphold yourself? Do you do the very things you're accusing him of doing? Take your time to examine your heart on this question.

Envy is insidious in a marriage. Do you want what you don't have? Do you see someone else who appears to have a happier marriage or a more attentive husband or a husband who gets things done or ... or ... or...? I'm sure you can finish the sentence for yourself. Discontent will suffocate any happiness you may have in your marriage. Don't entertain those thoughts.

Slander of every kind. This word could also be translated "unkind speech." This, like malice, can take forms that are more hidden. Do you give your husband that look that lets everyone else know you're not happy? Do you cast a bad light on your husband when you talk about him to your friends? Do you try to make him look worse than he is by making his actions sound worse and yours sound justifiable? All of this is slander.

APPLICATION

Look again at 1 Peter 2:1 and the list of things you must "rid yourself" of. Think through each of the sins listed there, and ask God to uncover what you can't see.

By now I'm sure you're asking: how do I actually get rid of these things? As you examine your life, confess your sins to God. Be thorough. Pray Psalm 139:23–24(NLT): "Search me, O God, and know my heart; test me and know my anxious thoughts. Point out anything in me that offends you, and lead me along the path of everlasting life."

Imagine yourself sitting in a chair, and Jesus comes over to wash your feet. As He does, picture all of the sins you have confessed draining out of you. Thank Him as He cleanses each one away. Now ask Him to lead you. Our next verse in 1 Peter 2 is a wonderful pursuit to start reflection on now: "Like newborn babies, crave pure spiritual milk, so that by it you may grow up in your salvation, now that you have tasted that the Lord is good." You wouldn't give a baby dirty water to drink. You wouldn't even give a newborn diluted milk; you wouldn't want any child to drink anything except pure milk. Think about what that means in your life: Pure. Crave purity, and ask God to lead you in the way everlasting, and fill you with pure spiritual milk.

It may be that through this exercise you realize you are holding on to anger and unforgiveness. If that is the case, you will find we focus more on these issues in Part 2, on Freedom through Forgiveness 1–5 and Freedom from Anger 1–2.

#12 PREPARING TO BE A LIVING STONE

1 Peter 2:4–10:

[4] As you come to him, the living Stone—rejected by humans but chosen by God and precious to him— [5] you also, like living stones, are being built into a spiritual house to be a holy priesthood, offering spiritual sacrifices acceptable to God through Jesus Christ. [6] For in Scripture it says:

"See, I lay a stone in Zion,

a chosen and precious cornerstone,

and the one who trusts in him

will never be put to shame."

[7] Now to you who believe, this stone is precious. But to those who do not believe,

"The stone the builders rejected

has become the cornerstone,"

[8] and,

"A stone that causes people to stumble

and a rock that makes them fall."

They stumble because they disobey the message—which is also what they were destined for. [9] But you are a chosen people, a royal priesthood, a holy nation, God's special possession, that you may declare the praises of him who called you out of darkness into his wonderful light. [10] Once you were not a people, but now you are the people of God; once you had not received mercy, but now you have received mercy.

ARE YOU PREPARED to be a "living stone"? What in the world does that even look like? Imagine the grandest stone building you've ever seen. A tall castle or perhaps a huge cathedral with a bell tower reaching into the sky. God is building a house for Himself, the true church. Christ is the cornerstone, the original "living stone." If we have new life in Christ, then we also are living stones and being built into God's building. We are part of Him and the place where He dwells. A spiritual house. Being built to be a holy priesthood. Do any of those words describe you? Yes, they all do. What will change if you think of yourself that way? This is *God's* house, not your house. Somehow, I always thought it was my house I was building, and you were building yours. In this passage, it is God's house.

How does one prepare?

I am a hiker. During the long winter, I can't hike as much, so as spring approaches, I need to get ready to start again. When I want to get ready for hiking season, I exercise regularly with stretches especially designed to strengthen the muscles in my legs. I go on more walks, go on smaller but strenuous hikes, and increase the difficulty and length little by little. I walk up the big hill near my home, rather than going around on the road. I gather my supplies. I make plans for dates, times, and locations to hike, and I make the arrangements.

How does this translate spiritually? It requires me to change my thinking. I have to exercise with specific soul formation in mind: spiritual direction, Bible study, mentoring, practicing my new listening skills, silence, solitude, prayer, and praise. I watch for opportunities to grow or help someone else grow. I make plans; I don't just expect it to happen without my effort.

Jesus, the Living Cornerstone, is precious to you if you believe.

You must believe Jesus can change you and your situation; He has to be the cornerstone of your faith. Where there is unbelief in your life, you will stumble. Reflect for a moment: is Jesus the cornerstone of all areas of your life? Maybe you try to prop yourself up with other supports; and you find yourself in a house of cards. Ask the Holy Spirit to reveal them to you and smash them down one by one. Resolve right now that Jesus is going to be the cornerstone of all your faith. Once you are solid in Him, you will no longer stumble, and you also can understand why other people do. Pray that those who do not know Him, or who have turned to unbelief, will recognize who He is so they can stop stumbling and submit to Him.

"You are a chosen people, a royal priesthood, a holy nation, God's special possession." Think through each of these incredible words. When you think of God's chosen people, do you immediately think of the Israelites in the Old Testament? All of these phrases describe you, too. *Chosen*: you are hand-picked by God. *Royal*: you are a daughter of the King. *Priest*: you are set apart for a purpose in

God's house. *Special possession*: like a cherished, priceless jewel. *You!* Are you ready to praise Him? He called you out of darkness, into His wonderful light. Whenever I read these words, I think of a prisoner chained in a cold, dark cell. Suddenly the wall starts to break and a brilliant light shines through. A voice beckons you to come out; a hand reaches in to rescue you. This is what God has done.

APPLICATION

What does God want to show you about yourself? Are you wandering in your heart or your actions?

What things are there that you can do if you have the opportunity? Ask God to open those doors.

Are you a sheep with one eye on the door, inside, yelling "Let me escape"? Are you busying yourself so you don't have to look, or have an excuse not to do what God is telling you? Ask God to give you the heart to obey.

What are the functions of a stone?

What changes if you start thinking of yourself as part of God's spiritual house?

What is your action plan?

How do you respond to our God who has made you one of His chosen ones?

In what ways have you noticed that God has set you apart to be His special possession?

#13 LIVING THE DIFFERENCE

1 Peter 2:11–12:
[11] Dear friends, I urge you, as foreigners and exiles, to abstain from sinful desires, which wage war against your soul. [12] Live such good lives among the pagans that, though they accuse you of doing wrong, they may see your good deeds and glorify God on the day he visits us.

"GOD IS MORE concerned about our character than our comfort."[4]

Are there times when you feel like an alien and stranger in your own house? I know I do. With my husband's addictions, our lives are headed down two different paths. Sometimes it seems as though I don't belong in his world. It is good during those times to remember that our citizenship is in heaven. We are indeed "temporary residents and foreigners" on this earth, so it shouldn't surprise us when others who don't know Christ are pursuing goals that are so different from our own.

The problem is, we used to live in that world too. Even though we are new creations, and even though we are citizens of heaven, we need to live in this world, and all those sinful pleasures that we once indulged in are still here. Commercials still tell us we "need" to have certain products to be truly happy. Our friends and family are still the same people, doing those things we used to do and enjoy. There's no point in denying that some things are still appealing, even if many of our old sin habits are not (thank the Lord). "Abstain from sinful desires, which wage war against your soul." Keep away, separate, don't go there. Don't put yourself into the middle of temptation. Even though it's something that others may think is fine, you know for you it's not fine.

An example from my own life is shopping. I used to love to shop and even just to browse. I grew up in a big city, and going to the mall was a regular pastime for me and my friends. When I gave my life to the Lord, I began to realize I was feeding a monster by browsing among the stores. Envy, greed, and covetousness were fires being

---

4. Charles R. Swindoll, *The Quest for Character* (Portland: Multnomah Press, 1987), 176.

stoked by this regular habit. I needed to change my lifestyle to obey God's command to abstain from sinful desires, for they were indeed causing a war within me. Like the old story, it feels like two wolves fighting in my soul. The one who wins is the one I feed. I could no longer feed the desire to own things. So I stopped going to the mall unless I specifically needed to buy something, and then I went only to that store. I made shopping lists and stuck to them. When something caught my eye, I'd steer away (I still have to do that). I went for walks outside rather than down the aisle of a mall. I only shopped once a week on a certain day and got everything on that day. It was tough, but I did it, and now shopping doesn't have the same allure it once did.

Why do this? Apart from ridding your life of sin and disobedience to God, there is another reason: "Live such good lives among the pagans [unbelievers] that, though they accuse you of doing wrong, they may see your good deeds and glorify God on the day he visits us." It is true people aren't going to understand. They will tell you you're nuts and even wrong. What do you expect in a culture that continually approves of doing whatever feels good? What God's Word tells us to do is to live good lives—consistent lives, that align with our words. Over time, although others may still scoff or malign you, they will see your life. If your sin is replaced by good deeds, they'll notice, and God will get the glory.

APPLICATION

What sinful desires linger from your old life?

What do you need to do to abstain?

What good deeds can you implement in your life to replace these desires?

Set an action plan for your life of good deeds and glorifying God.

#14 SUBMISSION TO AUTHORITY

1 Peter 2:13–19:

¹³ Submit yourselves for the Lord's sake to every human authority: whether to the emperor, as the supreme authority, ¹⁴ or to governors, who are sent by him to punish those who do wrong and to commend those who do right. ¹⁵ For it is God's will that by doing good you should silence the ignorant talk of foolish people. ¹⁶ Live as free people, but do not use your freedom as a cover-up for evil; live as God's slaves. ¹⁷ Show proper respect to everyone, love the family of believers, fear God, honour the emperor.

¹⁸ Slaves, in reverent fear of God submit yourselves to your masters, not only to those who are good and considerate, but also to those who are harsh. ¹⁹ For it is commendable if someone bears up under the pain of unjust suffering because they are conscious of God.

FIRST PETER 2:13–25 is about submission, and begins with the example of submission to governing bodies. We know from Romans 13:1–2 that God establishes authority, and Paul is urging us to submit to the legitimate authority in place over us. Indirectly, disobeying human authority is disobeying God—but Paul instructs us that we must always do what is right (Romans 13:2–3). This is a pretty volatile topic during the time we live in; but at the time Paul wrote this, the emperor was Nero—a godless leader if ever there was one. Of course, obedience to any authority must never be in violation of the law of God. (See Acts 4:18–19 for an example.)

Work the message of these verses through your own life situation, adding each aspect through every area like ingredients in a cookie recipe. Who are the authorities in your life? God, your church, your boss, your mayor, local government representatives, and those in higher governmental positions. I'm sure you can think of others. Be honest; are you someone who has trouble submitting to authority? If you are, it may rub you the wrong way when an authority figure tells you what to do. If this is the case, then don't fool yourself into thinking you are perfectly submissive to God's authority. The earthly authorities are put into place by Him.

Look at verse 15: "It is God's will that by doing good you should silence the ignorant talk of foolish people." More than once, I have prayed, "Lord, silence the ignorant talk of my foolish husband." God will answer, but it is accomplished by doing good, which is God's will for you.

"Live as free people [not slaves], but do not use your freedom as a cover-up for evil." Have you ever known anyone who does this? I have met Christians who think it's okay for them to do all kinds of things that are contrary to God's Word because they are under grace and not law. Jesus did not come to abolish the law, and He does not want us to pretend He did. That's what this verse means.

Next, Peter goes on to talk about slaves. These truths resonate with me, because often I feel like a slave to my husband, who at times is like a "harsh master," always critical and demanding. How are you to submit in this case? "With all respect, not only to those who are good and considerate, but also those who are harsh." Wrap your mind around that. God is asking you to treat your husband with respect, even if he's harsh. Yes, he's not your master in the strictest sense of the word, but he is in authority over you, placed there by God. You may feel you are being treated unfairly, but verse 19 speaks to that: "It is commendable if someone bears up under the pain of unjust suffering because they are conscious of God." This is not talking about enduring suffering because you've done something wrong, but because of doing good. Do you have any circumstances like that in your life?

One of the problems I face consistently is doing whatever I can to make sure my husband doesn't get angry. A good reminder is 2 Timothy 1:7: "The Spirit God gave us does not make us timid, but gives us power, love and self-discipline." My fear does not come from God. At all. It comes from the enemy (Satan, not my husband), and I can reject it. And I can grab hold of what God *did* give me—a spirit of power, of love, and of self-discipline. I can *ask* for it; and I have. So can you.

APPLICATION

What authority do you have trouble respecting? What authority do you have no trouble with? What is the difference?

Confess to God your areas of rebellion (the opposite of submission), and ask Him to show you how you can change disrespect to respect.

Are there areas in your life where you may be using your freedom in Christ as a cover-up for evil? How will you change this?

Why do you think verse 16 is in the middle of a discourse on submission to masters?

In what ways do you struggle or suffer for doing what is right?

Ask God to give you what you need to endure. Ask Him to replace your fear with power, with love, and with self-discipline. How will having these affect your responses to authority?

How can you implement them?

#15 YOUR CALLING

1 Peter 2:19–21:

¹⁹ For it is commendable if someone bears up under the pain of unjust suffering because they are conscious of God. ²⁰ But how is it to your credit if you receive a beating for doing wrong and endure it? But if you suffer for doing good and you endure it, this is commendable before God. ²¹ To this you were called, because Christ suffered for you, leaving you an example, that you should follow in his steps.

"TO THIS YOU were called, because Christ suffered for you, leaving you an example, that you should follow in his steps." I doubt you ever thought about suffering as a calling. Neither did I. But it's there, in the Bible. Let's probe that a bit deeper.

What is a calling? Romans 8:28 is an oft-quoted promise: "in all things God works for the good of those who love him." Many people stop there, but that's not the end of the sentence. The statement continues, "who have been called according to his purpose." God has a purpose for you, and His calling is His summons to you to fulfill it. Your suffering has a purpose. This is worthy of further study if you are unclear. The idea you need to grasp today is that your unjust suffering is actually what God has called you to, part of His purpose for you. You may need to sit with that thought for a few minutes.

We know Jesus is calling us to follow Him; "Take up your cross daily and follow me" (see Luke 9:23). This looks different for each individual; we each must respond in our own heart and live it out in our own life. The standard, although it may look harder for some than for others, is really the same for all: "For whoever wants to save their life will lose it; but whoever loses their life for me will save it" (Luke 9:24). Even Jesus had a purpose and calling. He said many times that He only came to do the will of the Father. He left us with an example, so we should not think that something is wrong with our Christianity if we are suffering. As a matter of fact, something is wrong if we never suffer. (See 2 Timothy 3:12–13.)

Jesus is our example (1 Peter 2:21), and the expectation is that we will follow in His steps. Steps that lead to the cross. Probably not to physical death; but death to the rule and reign of self in our lives. Suffering is purging us, rooting out and ridding us of our self-sins (self-indulgence, self-centeredness, and self-righteousness, to name a few), so that we can move forward in our pursuit of Christlikeness.

APPLICATION

In what ways are you enduring unjust suffering as a "calling"?

Ask the Holy Spirit to reveal to you if there are ways you're suffering that He has not called you to. Are there ways you have self-inflicted suffering God never intended?

How does it change your perspective to know that your situation is something God has called you to?

#16 JESUS AS OUR EXAMPLE

1 Peter 2:21–25:

²¹ To this you were called, because Christ suffered for you, leaving you an example, that you should follow in his steps.

²² "He committed no sin,

and no deceit was found in his mouth."

²³ When they hurled their insults at him, he did not retaliate; when he suffered, he made no threats. Instead, he entrusted himself to him who judges justly. ²⁴ "He himself bore our sins" in his body on the cross, so that we might die to sins and live for righteousness; "by his wounds you have been healed." ²⁵ For "you were like sheep going astray," but now you have returned to the Shepherd and Overseer of your souls.

JESUS COMMITTED NO sin, and no deceit was found in His mouth. First things first—search your heart, and examine what part of your suffering is your responsibility. None of us can say that, like Jesus, we have committed no sin. Each of us has. Have you sinned in your response to anger? Do you fear or worry, doubting God? Have you failed to show love to your husband? What about deceit? It's easy to justify a small measure of deception in our marriages, maybe not telling the whole truth or withholding information or worse. Jesus's example is "no deceit in his mouth." How pure is your mouth? Jesus never deceived anyone. It's possible to deceive without saying anything, like hiding something you purchased or not telling your husband something because you think it'll cause a fight. Be very careful here; God needs to guide your actions, not fear or your own efforts in self-protection.

"When they hurled their insults at him, he did not retaliate; when he suffered, he made no threats." I am sure at some time you've been insulted, threatened, accused, verbally abused, or disrespected. The word translated "insulted" could mean any of those things. We know all of those happened to Jesus. And what was His response? "He did not retaliate." You may be thinking, *Yes, but He's God, and I'm not.* While that's true, God is not going to ask us to do something that He is not going to give us the strength and the power to do through His

Holy Spirit that lives in us. *His life is in you, and you can do it!* He did not make threats as He suffered. He surely could have. He didn't say, "You'll be sorry" or "I'll leave and never come back." He could have called down ten thousand angels to wipe out His enemies. But He did not. He didn't do anything to get back at them; if He had, He would not have gone to the cross.

What did He do instead? "He entrusted himself to him who judges justly." He entrusted Himself to God. This is a choice you have to make: Will you retaliate, relying on your own wisdom, your own strength, your own words, to get back at the one who is making you suffer? Or will you follow in Jesus's steps and entrust yourself to the One who is the Judge? You know He loves you thoroughly; you know He knows what you are going through. He is asking you: "Do you trust Me?"

Jesus Himself bore your sins in His body on the tree, so that you might die to sins and live for righteousness. Are you ready to do this? He heals your emotional and spiritual pain through His wounds. Are you ready to accept this healing? It's done (note the past tense). You are already righteous positionally before God; He has given you new life. Will you take it and live it?

You were a sheep led astray, but now you have returned to your Shepherd. Trust Him to oversee your soul.

APPLICATION

What sins have you committed, that are a contributor to your unjust suffering?

Have you sinned in your response to anger? Do you fear or worry, doubting God? Have you failed to show love to your husband? What about deceit? How pure is your mouth?

Pray Psalm 139:23–24 (NLT): "Search me, O God, and know my heart; test me and know my anxious thoughts. Point out anything in me that offends you, and lead me along the path of everlasting life."

In what ways do you retaliate?

In what ways do you need to entrust yourself to the One who judges justly?

If Jesus is asking, "Do you trust Me?" how do you answer?

In what ways do you need to die to sin and live for righteousness?

Make a chart in your journal listing your sins on the left and what you want to replace them with on the right.

Write a prayer to the Lord accepting His gift of healing for your specific needs. Visualize yourself receiving a healing balm from Him and apply it to your heart.

#17 INSTRUCTIONS FROM PETER FOR WIVES

1 Peter 3:1-2:
¹ Wives, in the same way submit yourselves to your own husbands so that, if any of them do not believe the word, they may be won over without words by the behaviour of their wives, ² when they see the purity and reverence of your lives.

FIRST PETER 3:1 states, "Wives, in the same way submit yourselves to your own husbands." What way? The 1 Peter 2:13-25 way. The way Jesus exemplified. As Peter described unjust suffering and Christ as our example of how to respond, in the same way, wives are to be submissive to their husbands. Even the unfair ones and the unjust ones. Even the harsh ones. Why? "So that, if any of them do not believe the word, they may be won over." If your husband isn't a believer, you are to submit as Christ did; but any husband, Christian or not, can at times be harsh, unfair, or unjust. No matter what your situation, submission is God's calling for you.

I think I need to add something more at this point about submission. Knowing when to submit and recognizing when your husband is asking you to do something immoral is a challenge. We should never submit to something that is immoral and against God's Word. Our first authority is Christ, and we always submit to Christ above all. Here, Peter calls his audience to also submit to earthly authorities for the sake of the gospel. To submit is to yield to the power or authority of another. I love this quote from the NIV Women's Study Bible: "Submission means to put all of yourself—understandings, knowledge, opinions, feelings, energies—at the disposal of a person in authority over you. This never means subjecting yourself to abusive tyranny, nor does it suggest mindless acquiescence to the whims of another. It is the yielding of humble and intelligent obedience— without suggestion of inferiority or worthlessness. A wife's deference to her husband is a duty owed to the Lord. A wife's submission is not as much to her husband, a mere man, *as it is to God and his plan for marriage*" (emphasis added).

Submission doesn't diminish your significance, for you know God would not do that. He created you uniquely, with skills and abilities to complement your husband in the partnership of marriage. Jesus is our example, and there was nothing about Jesus's submission that somehow made Him *less* than the people He submitted to. He was Master and Lord, but He chose to submit; to give up His rights voluntarily. Submission is yielding to another person's will, so when there is conflict, we choose to give up our rights, as long as we continue to do what is right in God's eyes. Submission does not imply that we are less important or inferior. Philippians 2:5–11 speaks of Jesus as One who "made himself nothing." It was His choice, and God is calling you to follow in His steps.

It would be appropriate at this point to say something about abusive relationships. I am neither a counselor nor a theologian; I can only write to you what I read in the Scripture. If you are in an abusive relationship, seek professional help for your situation. Sometimes the best way to effect change in your marriage is to remove yourself from your husband for a time. I trust that if this is what God has for you, He will guide you. Ask Him for wisdom, and do not doubt what He gives you (see James 1:5).

Verse 1 says that husbands will be won over "without words," not by your preaching or correcting or defending yourself. Do you often yield (submit) to your husband's will but make sure he knows you're unhappy about it or let him have an earful about why you don't want to? "Without words" has been a very difficult lesson for me. Especially when he wants to rail at me about why I'm wrong. Defending myself has always been my first response, often without even thinking about it. Why does he get to present his point of view without hearing mine? I am not talking about giving him the silent treatment, with anger coming through in every non-verbal way possible. "Without words" means choosing to submit and not say *anything* that would discredit the gospel and our witness to our husband of a life transformed by Christ. This is still a lesson I am learning.

Look back to 2:15: "It is God's will that by doing good you should silence the ignorant talk of foolish people." My husband's talk is often ignorant of who I am, and when he is inconsiderate of my feelings, he is foolish. God's Word says that in this situation we are to do good.

Doing good—what is that? All the things we have already been learning: Preparing your mind, setting your hope fully on God, showing self-control, entrusting yourself to His justice, loving deeply. Bearing up under the pain of unjust suffering. Just like Jesus: "When they hurled their insults at him, he did not retaliate; when he suffered, he made no threats. Instead, he entrusted himself to the One who judges justly" (1 Peter 2:23)

Do not retaliate, make no threats; trust God.

Don't forget, 1 Peter 2:21 says, "To this you were called, because Christ suffered for you, leaving you an example, that you should follow in his steps." Your calling. This present situation with your marriage is a calling.

In the book *Valley of Vision*, which is a collection of Puritan prayers, the selection titled "Christian Calling" is about suffering; "Let me not overlook the Hand that holds the rod."[5] It is the Lord who calls you, and it is He who is using your suffering to refine you. When I read this, the words "You are my fortress" come to mind. I picture the image of a child (me) being rescued and brought into a fort, enclosed in Jesus's arms, and He whispers, "It's okay now, you're safe. No one can hurt you. No one can get you."

"Lord, why am I still afraid?" I ask. Then I understand: it's because I don't believe Him. Not really. I look again to my example, the One who suffered for me, and I regain my peace.

APPLICATION

Does it make you angry to know that God is calling you to submission? Take some time, examine your heart on this, and bring what you find before the Lord. Consider the question, "How would Jesus submit in my situation?" Ask the Holy Spirit to purify your thoughts as you think through the answer

---

5. *The Valley of Vision*, 50.

What will it mean for you to submit "without words"?

What words are your go-to when you resist submission? Take time to write them down, and then go back and write replacement words beside them. Or write "no words" in those situations where you know you must say nothing. Ask the Holy Spirit to remind you as each situation arises.

Close your eyes, and picture yourself in the middle of a battle, and the Lord running to carry you to safety from your enemies. Who are your enemies? Are they fear, anger, worry, or other things? Remember, your husband is not your enemy.

Find promises from God's word that you can write out to remember during times of hardship. Keep this list with you to review often.

Reflect on these words from Mother Teresa: "Be living expressions of God's kindness; kindness in your face, kindness in your eyes, kindness in your smile. Kindness."

#18 PURITY, REVERENCE, AND INNER BEAUTY

1 Peter 3:1–4:
[1] Wives, in the same way submit yourselves to your own husbands so that, if any of them do not believe the word, they
may be won over without words by the behaviour of their
wives, [2] when they see the purity and reverence of your lives.
[3] Your beauty should not come from outward adornment,
such as elaborate hairstyles and the wearing of gold jewellery
or fine clothes. [4] Rather, it should be that of your inner self,
the unfading beauty of a gentle and quiet spirit, which is of
great worth in God's sight.

FIRST PETER 3 explains how husbands are won over by godly wives:
"when they see the purity and reverence of your lives." I thought: I have
to be pure and reverent *first*. Are you? Would your husband say that?

Purity and reverence come from pure hearts, pure living, pure
speech. Are you closer than you used to be? Not adorning yourself to
be beautiful, but "the unfading beauty of a gentle and quiet spirit."
Are you gentler, calmer, quieter? Then praise God that He's trans-
forming you! If your truthful answer is "not much," then ask Him to
change and remake you on the inside, and watch for opportunities to
demonstrate this change.

To give context on verse 3 and "outward adornment," Dorothy
A. Lee, in her book *The Ministry of Women in the New Testament*,
states: "The instructions on women's appearance, however distaste-
ful to modern sensibilities, challenge the expectation of wives to be
ornaments for their husbands, status symbols whose values lies in
their physical attractions. For 1 Peter, their true value is an ethical
and spiritual one, grounded in their actions for love and justice."[6]
Peter is freeing wives from social and cultural pressures to instead
focus on becoming more like Christ.

For us today, our beauty should not come from what we do for
the outside, but what we do for the inside. That's good (for me) because I'm not young anymore, and I was never what anyone would

---

6. Dorothy A. Lee, *The Ministry of Women in the New Testament: Reclaiming the Biblical Vision for Church Leadership* (Grand Rapids: Baker Academic, 2021), 143–144.

call beautiful. I remember how I obsessed over outward beauty when I was young—makeup, perms, trendy clothes, attention-drawing jewellery—all to be noticed. I wanted to be what society told me was beautiful. I wanted to be appealing to men for all the wrong reasons.

There is nothing wrong with taking care of yourself, and I'm not suggesting it is more holy to let yourself go and not care about your appearance. However, if the focus is always on how you look, there's a problem—one that Peter brings out in this text. Your focus should be on the inner self and allowing your inner beauty to be a testimony to what God has been doing in your life and to point your husband to the gospel.

How long did I spend in those days trying to beautify myself every morning? Far longer than I took to work on "the unfading beauty of a gentle and quiet spirit." I don't remember when I stopped wearing makeup or worrying about trendy clothes; but I do recall that I made a decided effort to change my focus. I asked myself, "What if I spent an hour with the Lord and fifteen minutes getting myself ready in the morning, rather than the other way around?" I wouldn't have believed it then, but now I know that it is possible.

In contrast to outward beauty, gentleness and a quiet spirit reflect "unfading beauty." Gentle and quiet are not words anyone would have ever used to describe me in the past. The changes in me have all been God's doing; He works in my heart, and I cooperate. Not just showing a manufactured gentleness, while biting back a sharp retort; not just a pretense of quiet while inside I'm fighting to stifle a frustrated scream. No, it's true inner calm and deep peace that produces the "gentle and quiet spirit, which is of great worth in God's sight." I wish I could say this is my permanent condition; but God is still working on me. I do know that I am a very different person than I was in the past.

The Lord is telling us our focus needs to be on the inside more than on the outside. What is there that makes a woman ugly or beautiful? When you look deeply into the eyes of a physically unattractive person and see deep love gazing back at you, that face suddenly becomes the most beautiful face in the world to you. That's what I long for people to see in me.

APPLICATION

In what ways do you demonstrate purity and reverence in your life that your husband can see?

In the Amplified Bible, verse 2 states, "when they see your modest and respectful behavior [together with your devotion and appreciation—love your husband, encourage him, and enjoy him as a blessing from God]." What do you need to change to put this into practice? Be specific. Ask the Holy Spirit for ideas if you can't come up with any. Start small, but don't stay there; work toward a true and pure love for him. Start by listing the ways you are thankful for him.

How much time do you spend working on your inner beauty compared to your outer beauty?

Is the Holy Spirit prompting you to change? Write out specific ways you can do that, starting today.

#19 INNER BEAUTY AND SUBMISSION

1 Peter 3:1–5:
¹ Wives, in the same way submit yourselves to your own husbands so that, if any of them do not believe the word, they may be won over without words by the behaviour of their wives, ² when they see the purity and reverence of your lives. ³ Your beauty should not come from outward adornment, such as elaborate hairstyles and the wearing of gold jewellery or fine clothes. ⁴ Rather, it should be that of your inner self, the unfading beauty of a gentle and quiet spirit, which is of great worth in God's sight. ⁵ For this is the way the holy women of the past who put their hope in God used to adorn themselves. They submitted themselves to their own husbands.

IN OUR LAST study, we looked at outer versus inner beauty; I want to continue to see how this change in our focus cooperates with God's work at remaking us on the inside. If we are not to focus on being beautiful on the outside, then how are we to make ourselves beautiful? The Amplified Version answers this in verse 4: "Let it be [the inner beauty of] the hidden person of the heart, with the imperishable quality and unfading charm of a gentle and peaceful spirit, [one that is calm and self-controlled, not overanxious but serene and spiritually mature] which is very precious in the sight of God."

What a worthy goal! The hidden person of the heart, God's girl, beloved and whole, faultless in His sight. As God is working in you on the inside, you will begin changing on the outside. Calmer. Gentler. Peaceful. Those things may seem very far from you now, but as you allow God to have His rightful place as King of your life, His reign and rule *will* change you. Self-control will become a notable character trait in your life. Serene instead of anxiety-ridden. As each situation comes along that triggers those old anxieties and you feel them rising up in you, give them to the Lord. Lay them in His hands, and take His peace into yours.

Peter ties this concept of inner beauty with submission beautifully. As we become the calmer, quieter, gentler person on the inside, we find ourselves also becoming less angry, less objectionable, less demanding. We become women who are more willing to yield our rights and submit to our husbands. In the New Living Translation, verse 5 says, "This is how the holy women of old made themselves beautiful. They put their trust in God and accepted the authority of their husbands." Peter doesn't tell us who he is specifically referring to, but the admonition to trust God is a good one for us to take to heart. Are you willing to allow God to do this work in you? Ask Him to continue His work in your life until it is completed. This unfading beauty, the gentle and quiet spirit within you will be the evidence of your submission to your husband and to the Lord.

I saw God working this out in my life in some very practical ways. At one point in my marriage, I remember asking God to give me space to deal with the big things as they happened so I could spend the time I needed with Him to respond properly instead of reacting badly to my husband. He answered faithfully, so that every time I discovered something my husband had done that was going to have a huge negative impact on our family, he was not around. Usually, he was at work; it gave me time to digest it, take it to the Lord, calm down, and ask for wisdom on how to handle it. God never failed in this. Try it!

The ultimate goal is spiritual maturity, which is very precious in God's eyes. This is what He wants for you, so He's going to do everything He can to move you toward maturity as long as you let Him. What are you waiting for?

APPLICATION

Where are you in the process of becoming gentler, calmer, and quieter?

Are you noticing how God is changing you? Think back to one year ago; how are you different in your attitude and responses to your husband?

Do you see your willingness to submit growing as you become more calm, gentle, and quiet in your spirit? What are some next steps for you? Ask God to give you practical ways that you can put this into practice.

What anxieties are you carrying around with you? Picture yourself kneeling before the cross, with each of your worries and concerns in bags on your back. One by one, take each of them and lay them down. Tell the Lord what it is you're putting down, and ask Him to take it and do His will in you. Go from easiest to hardest; and if you can't lift your burdens off of yourself, ask Him to do it. Journal your response to the Lord.

#20 DO NOT GIVE WAY TO FEAR

1 Peter 3:1–6:

¹ Wives, in the same way submit yourselves to your own husbands so that, if any of them do not believe the word, they may be won over without words by the behaviour of their wives, ² when they see the purity and reverence of your lives. ³ Your beauty should not come from outward adornment, such as elaborate hairstyles and the wearing of gold jewellery or fine clothes. ⁴ Rather, it should be that of your inner self, the unfading beauty of a gentle and quiet spirit, which is of great worth in God's sight. ⁵ For this is the way the holy women of the past who put their hope in God used to adorn themselves. They submitted themselves to their own husbands, ⁶ like Sarah, who obeyed Abraham and called him her lord. You are her daughters if you do what is right and do not give way to fear.

PETER HAS DISCUSSED submission and inner beauty. In verse 5, he returns to the theme of submission with the example of Sarah, and addresses fear. It is unclear which passage Peter refers to regarding Sarah, but his instruction to "do what is right" without fear is essential.

Now, why do you think Peter addresses fear?

I mulled this over for a long time. My husband isn't physically abusive, although I know down through the ages many women have been beaten physically and still are. Do I fear him? I realized, yes, I do. I fear his displeasure, his unkind remarks, and that *look*. I fear his anger, even if he doesn't lay a hand on me; I fear the silent treatment, the way he makes me feel small and worthless. Fear is a huge part of my life.

However, if we are doing what is right in God's eyes, we do not need to be afraid. Just as Jesus did, we must "entrust ourselves to him who judges justly" (1 Peter 2:23). I resonate with the Message rendering of verse 6, "You'll be true daughters of Sarah if you do the same, unanxious and unintimidated."

I reflected on the image of *peace flowing like a river*, and I thought, *It doesn't.* I know the Lord gives peace, but, in my heart, there's a dam with my husband's name on it. I recalled a massive boulder in the middle of a rushing river in an area where I often hike. Huge and unmovable, this rock is seven or eight feet high and splits the flow of the river downstream. Two fallen trees, one on each side, were wedged between the rock and the bank. The river flows around the rock and over the trees when it's high, but the water is hindered by the trees when it's low. It trickles over or under, but it slows down considerably. I felt the Lord telling me that the trees represented fear and doubt; and I thought the rock was Jesus. "No," He reminded me, "I am Living Water. The river represents Me." The rock represents my husband. This was a revelation; it was here that my fear and unbelief had lodged. Here the flow of Living Water is blocked. When His life flows strong in me, the two trees are covered but still lodged under the surface, firmly in place. Oh Lord; this is truth. Fear and doubt are both present in my life.

But I also read Psalm 13, and the Lord spoke again. "Oh Lord, how long will You forget me?" (NLT) is the opening line. "How long will you look the other way? How long must I struggle with anguish in my soul?" (verse 1). It goes on, and it all describes me. And at the end, it changes. "But I trust in your unfailing love. I will rejoice because you have rescued me" (Psalm 13:5). It's a done deal. Over. I am free. My life is in God's hands, and that includes my marriage. It has been done; God has done it, and I'm waiting for it to be worked out, to come through. Enemies are defeated.

Maybe fear has gripped you, and you are well aware of its presence. Maybe it's not something you saw before, but you are now recognizing fear's influence in your dealings with your husband. The only way to live without fear is to put your hope in God, to do what honours Him, and do not give in to feelings of fear that keep you from speaking or acting in a way that you know is right. Trust God. Ask the Holy Spirit to lead you, to give you words, to tell you when to speak and when to be silent. Truth needs to be spoken. Self-pity needs to be silent.

APPLICATION

Read over 1 Peter 3:4–6 again. Does it surprise you this ends with the word *fear*? Why do you think this is?

What would have to be out of your life for you not to be frightened in any way?

How has God been speaking to you about this? Do you trust Him?

Ask the Lord to show you what your next steps are, when fear assails you. Create an action plan, and pray that the Holy Spirit will show you how to implement it in your life.

#21 TELLING THE TRUTH

1 Peter 3:1–6:

¹ Wives, in the same way submit yourselves to your own husbands so that, if any of them do not believe the word, they
may be won over without words by the behaviour of their
wives, ² when they see the purity and reverence of your lives.
³ Your beauty should not come from outward adornment,
such as elaborate hairstyles and the wearing of gold jewellery or fine clothes. ⁴ Rather, it should be that of your inner
self, the unfading beauty of a gentle and quiet spirit, which
is of great worth in God's sight. ⁵ For this is the way the holy
women of the past who put their hope in God used to adorn
themselves. They submitted themselves to their own husbands, ⁶ like Sarah, who obeyed Abraham and called him her
lord. You are her daughters if you do what is right and do not
give way to fear.

I WANT TO stay a little longer with the concept of fear because I am
sure it's something many women struggle with. Much of what I've
called submission in the past was just me giving in to my husband
because I didn't want to fight. My goal was peace, and this was the
best way to get it.

Sometimes fear seems like a huge mountain, and I feel as if I've
been climbing a steep precipice. I pray and pray about the fear of my
husband's angry response to things I say or do. I feel like I am just
below the top of the ridge and can't see the other side. I feel like I am
climbing and clinging by my fingernails. But when I reach the top
and peek over, it is rocky cliffs below. I am at the top, but it is danger-
ous to go forward, and I can't go back. I think I'd rather have physical
fear than this emotional turmoil because at least if I fall to my death
physically, I'll be with Jesus. Can you relate? Fear-driven living is an
issue you may keep going back to that is trying to put you in bondage
and incapacitate you. It leaves you feeling vulnerable and unprotected. And it is really the sin of unbelief.

First Peter 2:15 was the hardest lesson to learn for me: "by doing
good you should silence the ignorant talk of foolish people." I asked,

"How, Lord, do I silence the ignorant talk of my foolish husband? What good must I do?"

And the Lord did not take long to answer: "Tell your husband the truth." How much his suspicions and accusations hurt. How unfounded they are. How I try to do everything right to avoid his anger which is undeserved. How he has to choose to trust me just as I have chosen to trust him.

Lord, please give me the grace not to be afraid.

I realized I had made an idol of peace in my home. It's a false peace; it's like a Pax Romana or the absence of conflict to control the pain. Like a little child who thinks everything's okay if Mommy and Daddy aren't yelling; yet there is a deeper dynamic going on that is always just below the surface. True peace comes from God and is deep, penetrating, long-lasting peace. He wants to give you that peace; He wants that peace to reign in your home.

My mentor has been in a difficult marriage to a non-Christian for over fifty years. She told me everything changed when she stopped being afraid of her husband. She said she was always afraid to tell him the truth because of his anger; but she said once she started to tell the truth, she realized that "the tiger had no teeth." Truth-telling honours God. Not sugar-coated, watered-down, or half-truths; not compromising or apologizing. Just plain truth. Can you do that? I like Joyce Meyer's advice: "Do it afraid." Remember, our example is Jesus; it doesn't tell us He said nothing but He didn't threaten or retaliate. Yes, we are encouraged to win our husbands over "without words," but there are also "words" times, and that's when our purity and reverence and our gentle and quiet spirit must come out.

I saw the precipice I was clinging to again, but this time, on the other side was a sunrise.

APPLICATION

Examine your life; are you giving in to your husband out of fear, but calling it submission?

What picture describes how you feel about your marriage?

What picture would you like to replace it with?

Are there situations when you are afraid to tell your husband the truth?

Are you compromising to keep the peace in your home?

Are you willing to tell him the truth?

#22 WHAT IS IT THAT YOU WANT MOST?

Romans 12:1–2:
[1] Therefore, I urge you, brothers and sisters, in view of God's mercy, to offer your bodies as a living sacrifice, holy and pleasing to God—this is your true and proper worship. [2] Do not conform to the pattern of this world, but be transformed by the renewing of your mind. Then you will be able to test and approve what God's will is—his good, pleasing and perfect will.

IF JESUS WERE standing in front of you, asking the question "What do you want me to do for you?" (see Mark 10:36, 51), what would your answer be? In our application today, I hope you'll take the time to work through that; but I'd like to tell you about my experience.

After giving it a lot of thought, my answer has become "Lord, save my husband." How much I have longed for his salvation! When Jesus asks what I want, that is my answer, always. But He has followed that with another question: "What if it costs you your life?" I know it's not physical life He's referring to. That actually wouldn't be all that difficult. But what if He means my life as I know it—the comfort, security, and all I value? Am I willing to give it up? Even as the question comes to mind, I know what my answer will be. With a deep sigh I say, "Yes, Lord. I did before, and I will again. I hope it actually works this time."

You see, many years ago when I discovered we were deeply in debt that my husband had incurred without my knowledge, I was faced with that same question. My honest answer then was no. But as God worked on my heart, I surrendered. I did lose everything—house, savings, reputation, respect—and took on a huge debt of over $200,000 (back in the times when houses cost only $50,000). My husband did come to faith in Christ and I rejoiced; but a few years later he fell back into sin, walked away from God, and had an affair. It occurred to me that I still resented God—for all that I went through and my husband's affair and return home without his recommitment to faith following that. I felt God had promised, but it never happened. Although I thought this was dealt with long ago, I realized I had held it against the Lord all this time.

Do you resent the Lord for the circumstances you find yourself in? You must deal with this; if you don't, you will never fully trust God.

In many ways, I felt like I was running. I came to a fork on the path and had to choose, so I turned left. Behind me came an avalanche of dirt and rocks—a wall collapsing. What is the fork, Lord? What is the wall?

Romans 12:1–2 tells us to present our bodies as a living sacrifice. What is the sacrifice? Is this what God is really asking of us? If I am losing my life for the Lord, I sense no fear. I know it's only through losing my life that I will find it. I also know He is not saying I will lose my marriage for my husband's salvation, only that I need to be willing. I am not willing to lose my marriage for my own selfishness, my work, my pride, or any other reason.

Back to 1 Peter 3. I am so thankful for the truth of this amazing passage. I hope you realize it's no accident you're in it right now. Remember His promise: by doing good, you'll silence the talk. Remember His command: submit to authority with respect even though you suffer for doing good (unjustly). Remember your example: Like Jesus: no deceit in your mouth; no sin; no retaliation for insults; no threats. "Entrust yourself to him who judges justly."

Ah! That's the fork; one path is giving in to fear, the other is toward faith even though I'm still afraid. Lord, I run to You. I hide in You (see Psalm 143). You deliver me from all my fears (see Psalm 34).

APPLICATION

Picture Jesus standing in front of you and asking, "What do you want Me to do for you?" Take some time and think about the answer to that. It may take a few surface answers before you get to the real thing. When you do, lay that desire in front of Him.

Now hear Him ask you, "What if it costs you your life?" Is your heart's desire something worth dying for?

What if it costs your comfort, your life as you know it, your relationships, everything?

Are you willing to be a living sacrifice? Sit with that before the Lord. Stay there until you can honestly say, "I delight to do Your will, O my God."

What is the fork in the road that God is bringing you to? What will you choose?

What wall does God want to collapse behind you?

#23 BEARING HIS SIN

1 Peter 2:23–3:1:

²³ When they hurled their insults at him, he did not retaliate; when he suffered, he made no threats. Instead, he entrusted himself to him who judges justly. ²⁴ "He himself bore our sins" in his body on the cross, so that we might die to sins and live for righteousness; "by his wounds you have been healed." ²⁵ For "you were like sheep going astray," but now you have returned to the Shepherd and Overseer of your souls.

¹ Wives, in the same way submit yourselves to your own husbands so that, if any of them do not believe the word, they may be won over without words by the behaviour of their wives.

CONTINUING TO LOOK at the example of Jesus, I want to focus on a different truth. First Peter 2:24 says, "He himself bore our sins in his body on the tree, so that we might die to sins and live for righteousness; 'by his wounds you have been healed.'" *This too is your example.* You must bear your husband's sin (in more than a "put up with" way), just as Jesus took your debt of sin: so your husband can die to sin and *live*. By the wounds you take, he will be healed.

As an example from my own life, I realized this was the case when I found out my husband had a credit card I knew nothing about. By the time I found it, he had accumulated $22,500 of debt. That was a staggering amount for our income level. I had a choice. I could wash my hands of him and let him deal with it; but if he didn't pay it off, we could lose our house. I had to absorb the debt into our family finances. I took on his debt—and that was when I finally realized that this was what Jesus did when He took my sin. My debt was paid; I didn't owe it anymore. And He was asking me to do the same for my husband.

Again, this is another way that wives are to submit. The NIV Study Bible note for 3:1 says, "[submit] is the same Greek verb as in 2:13 and 18, a term that calls for submission to a recognized authority. Inferiority is not implied in this passage. The submission is one of role or function necessary for the orderly operation of the home."

Forgiveness is not optional. You will find it's like an onion; you peel off one layer, but find yourself in the same place again and needing to peel off another layer. Don't assume, because you dealt with forgiveness earlier, that it's all done; it may be that God is exposing another level.

Once you have been able to fully forgive (and it will probably be a process), things will begin to change rapidly for your marriage. It doesn't mean everything will be better immediately, but *you* will be different. Barriers will fall when forgiveness is activated, and your husband will notice.

To use my previous metaphor of climbing to the top of a precipice, it's like reaching the top and starting down the other side; you've crossed over. After the glorious sunrise of freedom from the bondage of resentment and bitterness, the climb down will still be difficult but different.

APPLICATION

What are your husband's sins that you must bear?

What will that mean for you?

Have you forgiven him?

Ask the Holy Spirit to search your heart for unforgiveness. Don't rush this. If it helps you to have object lessons, write them down, and burn the paper. Ask God to prompt you quickly and make you extremely sensitive to His promptings when He reveals unforgiveness in you.

If unforgiveness is a problem for you, there are additional resources on forgiving in Part 2, Freedom through Forgiveness (studies 1–5). Please work through that before continuing with the study; once you return you may want to reread study 23.

#24 NO SLANDER OF ANY KIND

1 Peter 3:7–9:

⁷ Husbands, in the same way be considerate as you live with your wives, and treat them with respect as the weaker partner and as heirs with you of the gracious gift of life, so that nothing will hinder your prayers.

⁸ Finally, all of you, be like-minded, be sympathetic, love one another, be compassionate and humble. ⁹ Do not repay evil with evil or insult with insult. On the contrary, repay evil with blessing, because to this you were called so that you may inherit a blessing.

IN VERSE 7, Peter says to husbands, "In the same way". There is the same expectation for a husband to use Christ as his example in his relationship with his wife. He is to be considerate and treat his wife with respect as the "weaker partner". The Greek word used here, *asthenestero*, implies physical weakness and not a moral or intellectual inferiority. Peter reinforces this by saying that wives are co-heirs of God's gift of life. In the Message, Eugene Petersen puts it this way, "As women they lack some of your advantages. But in the new life of God's grace, you're equals."

As I mentioned in the first chapter, I always used to cringe when I read Bible passages telling me how husbands are supposed to act. I immediately assumed my husband was not going to act that way, because he no longer professes faith in Christ. Now that I have begun to recognize my ungracious thought patterns, I read verse 7 in a new way. My husband is actually very considerate, and I don't acknowledge or appreciate him as I should. Think about your own relationship with your husband. In what ways can you say he is considerate, thoughtful, and respectful toward you? Would your attitude toward him change if you focused on these things, rather than on the ways he is the opposite?

"Do not conform to the evil desires you had when you lived in ignorance" (1 Peter 1:14). Once God gives you an awareness of your sin and of what you need today, you are no longer ignorant. You can't go back. That applies in your marriage too. You can't go back to your old way of dealing with things. Please take the time to read again this entire passage, right from 1 Peter 1:13. Prepare your mind for action, be self-controlled, set your hope fully on God showing up. Be holy. Don't conform, don't slip back. Do not *slander*.

I was shocked when I realized how much I do that. My constant prayer is "Lord, change me." Peter refers to "slander of every kind." This is about more than just bad-mouthing; it also means no more slander inwardly. I realized my thoughts are slanderous. Every thought is tainted. My expectations: negative. My answers (in my head) to his words: negative. My attitude, approach, opinions: all very low, negative, slanderous. Looks, expressions, behind-his-back sneers, eyerolls, tongue-sticking. I pre-decide how he'll respond. *Lord, forgive us for how we disrespect our husbands!* How ugly. If the women of old made themselves inwardly beautiful, I just figured out how we make ourselves inwardly ugly.

But oh, how thankful I am that the Lord can take it away. On my knees, I asked God to renew my mind (see Romans 12:2). *Forgive me, Lord, for doing the things I accuse* him *of. Lord, make me really sensitive to this.*

But as always, it's important to replace what you have asked God to remove with something good. Peter says we are to "live such good lives among the pagans (unbelievers) that, though they accuse you of doing wrong, they may see your good deeds and glorify God on the day he visits us" (1 Peter 2:12). Let me personalize this. Though your husband accuses you of doing wrong, he will see your good deeds and glorify God. (Note: it doesn't say he'll apologize to you.)

Can you truly ask, "Lord, be glorified"? Ask Him to show you what good deeds you need to replace the bad. Here's some new ways to focus on being: live in harmony with your husband, be sympathetic toward him, love him as a brother (it will change things, trust me!), be compassionate toward him and humble. The Amplified Version puts it this way, "Be like-minded [united in spirit], sympathetic, brotherly, kind-hearted [courteous and compassionate toward each other as members of one household], and humble in spirit." The atmosphere has completely changed in my home since I took this to heart. The peace and calm that comes from like-mindedness seems to minimize the tension when there is disagreement. Although I don't always agree with my husband, I often don't argue anymore. It used to bother me that by withholding my viewpoint (which I always thought was right) meant that I affirmed he was right, or that he "won"; but the truth always comes out eventually. By doing this I showed him I was respecting his opinion, and over time he settled into a place of asking for mine.

"Do not repay evil (words, actions, look) with evil or insult with insult ... because to this you were called." (Again, there's that word *called*!) Ask the Lord to remake you, to help you prepare for this new way of acting.

The Amplified Version continues in verse 9, "never return evil for evil or insult for insult [avoid scolding, berating, and any kind of abuse], but on the contrary, give a blessing [pray for one another's well-being, contentment, and protection]; for you have been called for this very purpose, that you might inherit a blessing [from God that brings well-being, happiness, and protection]."

APPLICATION

What admonition(s) from the passage is God speaking most directly to you about?

Are you getting better? What measurable steps can you take to continue to improve?

What are the kinds of slander that you have a problem with? Take time to list them, and repent of each one. Think through what you will do instead in thoughts, words, or actions. Make a habit of immediately turning to God as soon as you have the slightest inkling of temptation.

What is one of the good actions listed in verses 8–9 that you can begin to practice?

Try making a list of what you love and appreciate about your husband. Don't stop until you have a full page, and then keep adding things as you think of them over the next few days.

Write out a blessing for your husband, and pray it each day for a week or longer. Try it! It can be transformational for you and for him.

#25 SANCTIFIED

1 Corinthians 7:10–17:

¹⁰ To the married I give this command (not I, but the Lord): a wife must not separate from her husband. ¹¹ But if she does, she must remain unmarried or else be reconciled to her husband. And a husband must not divorce his wife.

¹² To the rest I say this (I, not the Lord): If any brother has a wife who is not a believer and she is willing to live with him, he must not divorce her. ¹³ And if a woman has a husband who is not a believer and he is willing to live with her, she must not divorce him. ¹⁴ For the unbelieving husband has been sanctified through his wife, and the unbelieving wife has been sanctified through her believing husband. Otherwise your children would be unclean, but as it is, they are holy.

¹⁵ But if the unbeliever leaves, let it be so. The brother or the sister is not bound in such circumstances; God has called us to live in peace. ¹⁶ How do you know, wife, whether you will save your husband? Or, how do you know, husband, whether you will save your wife?

¹⁷ Nevertheless, each person should live as a believer in whatever situation the Lord has assigned to them, just as God has called them.

FIRST CORINTHIANS 7 is a chapter on marriage. If you have time, read the whole chapter, underlining those parts where God is speaking to you. Then, slowly read 1 Corinthians 7:10–17 again. This passage is about staying married to an unbeliever, for the unbelieving husband *has been sanctified* through his wife. Wow. That's a done deal, since it says "*has been*" sanctified. Your husband is sanctified through his marriage to you. But what if you're not sanctified in some area of your life (such as silent slander)? Are you blocking him from being sanctified because it comes through you? This is good evidence of what I've known for a long time; the Lord is going to work on *me first (and you) before we see evidence of His work in our husbands*. As His children, He wants to purify and sanctify us. Every time we go to Him complaining about our husbands, He points the finger at us and says,

"I see that sin in *you*." This is the spiritual principle of plankeye (see study 3). I wonder how much your rebellion and disobedience blocks your husband from being sanctified. This is something that must be brought before the Lord for a thorough searching and cleansing.

Note also verse 17: "Each person should live as a believer in whatever situation the Lord has assigned to them, just as God has called them." There's *called* again. When you complain to the Lord about your circumstances or expend a lot of energy trying to control things in your home, you may actually be in rebellion against God. Submitting to Him, surrendering your situation to His hands, and then doing only what He tells you is the only way to bring real and effective change.

Often, I see my marriage as a barren land; but the Holy Spirit is a river that flows through that land, nourishing the trees like the strong pillars of my marriage (faithfulness, home, children, family, jobs, church) and flowing out to feed the life that is further downstream (the future). The river pours over a precipice as a wide, straight waterfall, not as fast flowing, as those with more rocks, but constant. The Lord invites me to drink deeply. The waterfall is His love. I stand under, and it washes over me. I drink and drink. The pain, like cracks in a rock, becomes a water channel where the river pours out from me to my husband and family and to the others in my life.

APPLICATION

In what ways do you need to be sanctified that may be blocking your husband's sanctification? Write them down and confess them to the Lord. Offer yourself again to Him as His "instrument of righteousness" (see Romans 6), to work through you in your husband's life.

How does the knowledge of your husband being sanctified through you change things in you, your life, and your marriage?

Is God calling you to make a change? What is He asking of you?

Picture yourself in the scene described above. Let God's love wash over you like a waterfall. Sit silently (inner and outer) before Him, and allow yourself to be refreshed.

#26 REFRESH YOURSELF

I WANT TO take a bit of a breather for some self-care. After going through all of this truth, which may be paradigm-shifting for you (it was for me), I would like to take the time to sit with the Lord and allow Him to refresh you, to pour His love over you, to replenish your heart. After all, we aren't working through a *seven steps to a better marriage* program. Ultimately, although we hope our marriage improves, this Bible study is about God revolutionizing our lives so that we can be more like Him in the way we interact with our husbands.

Read and meditate on Isaiah 41:13.

"For I am the Lord your God
who takes hold of your right hand
and says to you, Do not fear;
I will help you."

Try this method of meditation: Read the verse slowly a few times. Contemplate its overall meaning. Go through each word in the verse, and look at it alone. Mull it over; think upon its meaning in the context. Chew on it until you are satisfied by its nourishment, and then move on to the next word. Once you are done, turn it into a prayer to the Lord.

Now do the same with Isaiah 40:11.

He tends his flock like a shepherd:
He gathers the lambs in his arms
and carries them close to his heart;
he gently leads those that have young.

Allow these truths to soak into you, as you take them for yourself as a prayer.

Lord, You hold me in Your hand. You hold my right hand. You carry me in Your arms. I am Yours. I am a chosen servant. A little lamb. Let me hear You whisper, "Do not fear. I will help you. The wind, earthquake, and fire have come and will come, but wait for Me and listen for Me. The silence is coming too." (See 1 Kings 19:11–12.)

Tell the Lord that you do fear, too much. Name your fears: rejection, failure, poverty, abandonment, pain; whatever they are. Perfect love casts out fear, His Word tells us (1 John 4:18). Ask the Lord to bring you this perfect love. Ask Him to take away your fear of love, and ask Him to send waves of His love over you. Contemplate Romans 5:5: "Hope does not put us to shame, because God's love has been poured out into our hearts through the Holy Spirit, who has been given to us."

Ask Him to let you feel this love being poured into you.

Take this promise and make it your own: "You deliver me from all my fears" (Psalm 34:4).

#27 RESPOND WITH BLESSING

1 Peter 3:8–14a:
⁸ Finally, all of you, be like-minded, be sympathetic, love one another, be compassionate and humble. ⁹ Do not repay evil with evil or insult with insult. On the contrary, repay evil with blessing, because to this you were called so that you may inherit a blessing. ¹⁰ For,

"Whoever would love life
and see good days
must keep their tongue from evil
and their lips from deceitful speech.
¹¹ They must turn from evil and do good;
they must seek peace and pursue it.
¹² For the eyes of the Lord are on the righteous
and his ears are attentive to their prayer,
but the face of the Lord is against those who do evil."
¹³ Who is going to harm you if you are eager to do good?
¹⁴ But even if you should suffer for what is right, you are blessed.

BACK TO 1 Peter again. How are we to embody all of the characteristics in 3:8–9? "Finally, all of you, be like-minded, be sympathetic, love one another, be compassionate and humble. Do not repay evil with evil or insult with insult." Maybe the answer is the next part of verse 9; not to reply to evil or insult in kind, but with the blessing: of well-being, contentment, and protection. To this you were called, so you can inherit this same blessing.

Peter here quotes Psalm 34, as if he is giving us his reasons for obeying the commands in verses 8 and 9. "For whoever wants to love life and see good days *must* keep her tongue from evil and her lips from deceitful speech" (feminine pronouns added). The Amplified Version expands on "good days": "[good—whether apparent or not] … tongue free from evil and her lips from speaking guile." Do you know what guile is? A common definition is "insidious cunning in attaining a goal; crafty or artful deception, duplicity." Does any of that describe you? Do you use cunning, craftiness, or creative deception to get your own way? How about duplicity? That is basically speaking or acting different ways to different people about the same matter. "Two-faced," we used to say. Are your dealings with your husband free from that? Is there any kind of manipulation in your dealings with him?

The quote from Psalm 34 continues in verse 11: "She must turn from evil and do good. She must seek peace and pursue it." (The Amplified says, "pursue it eagerly [actively—not merely desiring it].") "For the eyes of the Lord are on the righteous, and his ears are attentive to their prayer, but the face of the Lord is against those who do evil." Your fervent prayer should be, "Lord, look on me with favour, and eagerly answer my prayer."

In verse 13, Peter asks a thought-provoking question. "Who is going to harm you if you are eager to do good?" The one who doesn't believe it, that's who. Your husband may be like that, but are you? Give that some thought. Do you always have an expectation that his actions and words have a hidden motive; that he's not nice to you unless he wants something? When you think about what might happen in a situation, do you expect bad from him? If you don't believe he means good for you, then why do you expect him to believe that of you?

"Even if you should suffer for [doing] what is right, you are blessed." (And it's not certain that you will suffer!) You're blessed—favoured by God, even if your husband does question your motives. You're blessed especially when you suffer for doing what is right.

APPLICATION:

List the characteristics in this passage (verses 8–11), and put a star beside the ones that you most need to work on.

Spend time with the Lord, allowing Him to search your heart and point out where you need to change. Don't spend time in *self*-examination; let the Lord bring it to mind. He will. If you're having trouble getting started, hold each one before Him as a question: "What about this, Lord?" and then sit in silence listening for His answer.

Once you have identified what needs to change, spend a few moments concentrating on each one and asking the Lord to show you what you need to do. It may be that you need to ask forgiveness. If that's the case, don't shy away from it. Allow God to lead you.

#28 DON'T BE INTIMIDATED

1 Peter 3:13–14:
¹³ Who is going to harm you if you are eager to do good? ¹⁴ But even if you should suffer for what is right, you are blessed. "Do not fear their threats; do not be frightened."

IT SEEMS AS if we keep coming back to fear. This is for a few reasons: first of all, because fear can be so deeply rooted that it affects every area of our marriage; second, because Peter keeps bringing it up. Truthfully, as God works in our life, it's like peeling layers off of an onion. As each layer is stripped away, we always have to come back to the point we started, to allow the layer to fully drop away, and then we can begin on the next layer. For many of us, that point is our fear. Even if it isn't, Peter is bringing it up again, so we will too.

First Peter 3:14 says, "Do not be afraid or intimidated by their threats, nor troubled or disturbed [by their opposition]." That's the Amplified Version; the NIV says, "Do not fear their threats." This is a reference to Isaiah 8:12, which states, "Do not call conspiracy everything this people calls a conspiracy; do not fear what they fear, and do not dread it." The context in Isaiah is a warning not to follow the ways of people, instead "The LORD Almighty ... is the one you are to fear" (Isaiah 8:13). That's a tough one, because again you must respect and submit but not allow yourself to be intimidated. Is this a problem for you?

As I reflected on this, God gave me a picture. As I'm sure you have figured out by now, God speaks to me often through nature and will show me nature scenarios to communicate a truth to me. When I prayed, "I want to be free of this fear, Lord. All of my fears," the Holy Spirit showed me thick tree trunks in a dark forest. I prayed, "It's time we cut down the trees in the forest of fear, Lord. Let in the light for the little trees of good to grow." I started to enter the forest, but the Spirit pulled me away and lifted me up. I yelled, "No! No!" I looked back, and it was razed, only stumps visible in a large brown field. Why does it feel like loss? If they're gone, why am I still living in this place of fear? It doesn't feel like they're gone. I actually feel worse. Could it be because the familiar has just been ripped away from me?

My place of hiding, from which I needed to be delivered, had come to feel like safety? So many years of living in fear and shame that now I feel exposed? "Lord, when You remove the fear, please come and replace it with Yourself," I prayed. I still was confused. "What do You want, Lord? Why do I hurt?"

He answered, *"Let go."* Suddenly I was on that mountain again, at the top but on the other side, holding on for dear life.

"No! No! I can't! It took so long to get up here. I climbed and climbed. I struggled for thirty-five years. Let go?"

He repeated, "Let go!" What does it mean to let go? Of my husband, my marriage, my lifestyle?

My hopes and dreams? Of my plans for my future? "Of all of it," He gently whispered. "Let go."

I feel no peace. The Spirit gently reminds me to "seek peace and pursue it" (verse 11). How can I pursue peace? The Lord reminded me of the rich young ruler (see Matthew 19:16–22). Was this me? Am I really going to walk away and say no? This is Jesus's invitation to follow Him, and I'm refusing? *"Don't let me, Lord!"* I begged. In my vision, I fell at His feet. "You, Lord, only You." I know I'd rather feel pain of loss than separation from the Lord.

The Holy Spirit stayed with me; I felt His presence until I began to settle inside. It was then I realized that in order to stop pain, I had buried hope along with my other attachments. I see how it could happen. I asked the Father, "Lord, if the Forest of Fears is gone, can hope be planted anew?" His peace let me know that the answer is yes. I am transplanted into a Garden of Hope. Right now, I don't see it; but it's like new seeds planted along the edge of a river. As I wait to see more, they will grow. I searched for the hope from 1 Peter and reviewed all the Lord had taught. It finally came to me that I am to set my hope fully on the grace to be given me when Jesus Christ is revealed (see 1 Peter 1:13).

Once again at the top of the mountain, my way is shrouded in a band of fog. I'm descending into fog, but that's okay, it'll lift. I always knew I'd have to go back down; like Elijah after hearing the still, small voice (see 1 Kings 19), eventually it's time to "go back the way you came". I know I'm on the side of the sunrise I saw from the top. Hope.

And so I let go. I don't know what is ahead, but I know that if I fall, the Lord will catch me. That is enough.

APPLICATION

Read slowly the narrative of my experience. (Although this was a vision, not too long after I experienced it, I did actually find this physical mountain on Vancouver Island, and it was exactly as He had shown me.) Try and picture it in your mind, and ask the Holy Spirit to allow you to feel what I felt. It may be that He has another picture to show you; that's fine. Let the Holy Spirit lead your thoughts.

What is your forest of fear?

Is God ready to remove it but you're fighting Him? What seeds would He want to plant in a garden of hope?

Allow Him to lead, and don't rush away too quickly. Record your experience with Him so that you can remember and refer to it again.

#29 CHANGING YOUR EXPECTATION

1 Peter 3:13-14:
¹³ Who is going to harm you if you are eager to do good? ¹⁴ But even if you should suffer for what is right, you are blessed. "Do not fear their threats; do not be frightened."

ONE THING I knew would have to happen after all the Lord had shown me was that I would have to change my expectations of my husband. I must not assume when I interact with him that it's going to be bad; I must assume that it's going to be good, as the Lord promised. I also have to resolve not to keep returning to the sin of fearful expectations.

Review this point in your own mind. Do you expect bad from him, or good? When you plan to have a conversation with him, do you immediately assume he will be negative, argumentative, or combative? Ask God to show you how to enjoy your husband as a blessing from Him. "Do not conform to evil desires you had when you lived in ignorance" (1 Peter 1:14). Once you are aware of a sin, this verse applies. That he "may see your good deeds." (2:12). This is a show, not tell, situation. Remember the Lord's admonition, "without words" (3:1).

It may help to review your primary fears and find God's promise to answer them. Here are mine to help get you started:

My top five fears and God's answer:

Fear of rejection: God *will never* leave you (see Hebrews 13:5); He has chosen you and not rejected you (see Isaiah 41:9).

Fear of failure: All things work together for good (see Romans 8:28); He who began a good work in you will be faithful to complete it (see Philippians 1:6).

Fear of poverty: My God will supply all your needs (see Philippians 4:19).

Fear of abandonment: God will never forsake you (see Hebrews 13:5); God is with you always (see Matthew 28:20); God has rescued you (see Psalm 91:14); God delights in you (see Isaiah 42:1).

Fear of pain: God will not let your foot slip (see Psalm 121:3); Even though you walk through the valley of the shadow of death, you will fear no evil (see Psalm 23:4); God is your hiding place (see Psalm 32:7).

Remember that perfect love casts out fear (see 1 John 4:18). I have also heard it said that perfect fear casts out love. Don't let any fear linger. The forest is razed, and the trees are gone. Once you have eliminated your fear, you are free to change your expectation of your husband. You will change your response to him too, because you won't come toward him with your shields up, your defenses ready, your hand on your gun, so to speak. Allow the Lord to change and temper you.

APPLICATION

What are your fears? Spend time writing them out and finding promises of God to answer them. This, too, is a change in thinking.

What lies does Satan tell you about yourself? It's possible that many of these come out of your husband's mouth. Write down each lie, and beside it, write God's truth. Put this in a place where you can read it when you're tempted to believe the lies again. Just because your husband says you are stupid (or whatever) does not make it true.

What bad expectations do you have of your husband? Confess each one to God, and continue to do so throughout this coming week. Ask the Holy Spirit to make you especially sensitive to how your expectations are not honouring Him. Most of all, as you confess these, lay them down before the Lord, and pick up whatever He wants you to replace them with.

If you commonly expect your husband not to get things done, expect that he will. If you usually expect him to give an angry response, expect him to give a cheerful, loving response. Think through every one, and ask the Lord to intervene—and expect Him to answer.

#30 RESPONDING DIFFERENTLY IN PRACTICAL WAYS

1 Peter 3:15–18:

¹⁵ But in your hearts revere Christ as Lord. Always be prepared to give an answer to everyone who asks you to give the reason for the hope that you have. But do this with gentleness and respect, ¹⁶ keeping a clear conscience, so that those who speak maliciously against your good behaviour in Christ may be ashamed of their slander. ¹⁷ For it is better, if it is God's will, to suffer for doing good than for doing evil. ¹⁸ For Christ also suffered once for sins, the righteous for the unrighteous, to bring you to God. He was put to death in the body but made alive in the Spirit.

ONCE YOU HAVE worked through the expectations, this is a new (next) thing to think through; because you *will* encounter those looks, words, and actions again. Like the eye-rebuke when he gives you that look. If you are not to react with fear or intimidation, what will your response be? First, you need to test the atmosphere, like the temperature outside, and then dress appropriately (see the clothing of Christ, Colossians 3:12–14). When those situations come, you should assess and take what is necessary: Do you need to apologize? What is true? What do you need to learn? Then *dump the rest*. Do what you need to. Run to the Father and not to fear. Invite Him in, and stand together. Take His armour if needed, and choose the sword (Scripture) that fits. He is your shield. Stop fear from reseeding or even plowing a new rut. But please, don't stop what God is doing.

Remember these 1 Peter verses: do not fear their threats. Set apart Christ as Lord. Ask yourself who is Lord here? Be prepared to give an answer at the Lord's prompting. My go-to answer was always self-justification because it came from fear. What is yours? Do you need to prepare yourself to give an answer? The new answer/response must come from *hope*.

You may be thinking, "Wait, didn't you tell me to win him over without words?" Yes. However, there will come a time when it is appropriate to speak. Silence first, speaking second; I don't think Peter's instructions are in this order by accident. And this passage also cautions us to "do this with gentleness and respect." The right answer will always be given in a gentle and respectful way. Don't give in to fear of his threats or his anger

Again, it's like the river, from study #20, and this time I'm sitting on the rock in the middle, with the trees of fear and doubt lodged against the rock but the water has covered them. Although they are covered, they are still under the surface and disrupting the flow. But fear should be gone, right?

"Chop it up," I heard the Spirit whisper.

"I'm too weak, Lord," I replied.

"I will help you" came the calm assurance. So I did. With an axe in my hand and my imagination guided by the Holy Spirit, I chopped off fear of anger. Next, fear of the future. Then the fear of poverty, abandonment, failure, rejection. The pieces floated downriver and then over a huge waterfall.

I sat with the Lord at the top, looking over. I asked the Lord, "What is this waterfall?"

The Lord impressed upon me that the river was ministry, an outflow of His presence in my life. Preparing an answer for the hope you have applies to more than just your husband. I confessed my fear of launching into a new area of ministry; who did I think I was? It was then that I saw 1 Peter 3:15–18 in a new light: for others. If I'm teaching, I need to remember not to fear (verse 14); to set apart Christ as Lord; to be prepared to give an answer for my hope. And my hope for them, so that they too can have hope.

Although this was about the Lord giving me a way to minister to others, this admonition is also for you. The Lord will bring other women into your life, and you need to prepare an answer for the hope that you have. But do it with gentleness and respect, keeping your conscience clear so there's nothing to malign, nothing to undermine your testimony. Don't use your ministry to other women as a platform to air your griefs and slam your husband. Remember: Christ died for all those sins once and for all, the righteous for the unrighteous, to bring you to God. This is the response of a good conscience toward God (see 1 Peter 3:21).

APPLICATION

What are your current responses, and what do you need to change?

Think about one specific situation that happened recently. Putting yourself back in that place again, how could you have tested the temperature and dressed accordingly?

Colossians 3:12–14 gives us a list to clothe ourselves with, such as tender-hearted mercy, kindness, humility, gentleness, patience, bearing with him, forgiveness, and love. What did you need to take away? What should you have dumped?

What ways can you prepare for the next time?

What Scripture can you take to arm yourself with?

Put yourself into my vision. What has lodged in your heart that you cannot get rid of?

Ask the Lord to help you "chop it up". Ask Him what you are to do with all that He's teaching you, whom you are to share it with.

#31 THE HIGHER PURPOSE OF SUFFERING

1 Peter 4:1–6:

¹ Therefore, since Christ suffered in his body, arm yourselves also with the same attitude, because whoever suffers in the body is done with sin. ² As a result, they do not live the rest of their earthly lives for evil human desires, but rather for the will of God. ³ For you have spent enough time in the past doing what pagans choose to do—living in debauchery, lust, drunkenness, orgies, carousing and detestable idolatry. ⁴ They are surprised that you do not join them in their reckless, wild living, and they heap abuse on you. ⁵ But they will have to give account to him who is ready to judge the living and the dead. ⁶ For this is the reason the gospel was preached even to those who are now dead, so that they might be judged according to human standards in regard to the body, but live according to God in regard to the spirit.

I HAVE ALWAYS struggled with the meaning of 1 Peter 4:1; the part about suffering in your body and being done with sin. Is that really the case? I know that suffering helps to clarify what you really need versus what you want. I think that when you suffer, all the earthly pursuits don't look as important, and your priorities are reordered. The context in this passage is suffering for being/doing good and having Jesus's attitude. You are to "arm yourselves" with the same attitude, verse 1 tells us, which is one of the things you can do to "prepare your mind for action" (1 Peter 1:13). Once done with sin, the result is that you do not live the rest of your earthly life for evil human desires (see verse 2). There's nothing like persecution or suffering to sharpen your focus. "You have spent enough time in the past doing what the pagans choose to do" (verse 3). How much time do you spend doing what the world says you ought to be doing?

Are you prepared to live for Christ and not for yourself? Laying down your desires, even the good ones, for God's best? Your goal should be the ability to say, "I delight to do your will, O my God."

In the context of marriage, there's no beating around the bush. Remember Ruth with Naomi? Maybe these verses were even read at your wedding. How fitting this is for wives: "Don't urge me to leave or to turn back from you. Where you go I will go, and where you stay I will stay" (Ruth 1:16). This applies to the Lord Jesus first and then with your husband second; only with your husband you cannot truly say "Your gods will be my gods." You have to reserve that for Jesus alone. Ruth continues in verse 17, "Where you die I will die, and there I will be buried. May the Lord deal with me, be it ever so severely, if even death separates you and me." Wow. That's quite a vow. And it doesn't only apply physically. What separates you from your husband? Ask the Lord to bring the walls down and to reinforce what unites you.

There's a phrase in Psalm 18 that is all about the Lord giving strength. "You provide a broad path for my feet, so that my ankles do not give way. I pursued my enemies and overtook them; I did not turn back till they were destroyed" (Psalm 18:36–37). Again, this is about fear. Has a new one arisen with the thought of ministry or of suffering or of Ruth's vow? Don't let new fears lodge; cut them down as soon as they show up. "With your help I can advance against a troop; with my God I can scale a wall" (Psalm 18:29). Claim God's promise of strength.

APPLICATION

Are you prepared to live for Christ and not for yourself? Laying down your desires, even the good ones, for God's best? Your goal should be the ability to say, "I delight to do your will, O my God."

Read Ruth's vow again. What separates you from your husband? Ask the Lord to show you what you must do and to give you courage.

Again, visualize yourself sitting on the rock in the middle of the river. Are new logs of fear, doubt or discouragement lodging there, blocking the flow?

Ask the Lord for the strength and courage to knock them down as soon as they show up. You may have to get into the "flow" to do so. Remember Psalm 18, and ask God for strength.

#32 CLEAR MINDED AND SELF CONTROLLED

1 Peter 4:7–8:
⁷ The end of all things is near. Therefore be alert and of sober mind so that you may pray. ⁸ Above all, love each other deeply, because love covers over a multitude of sins.

FIRST PETER 4:7 says, "The end of all things is near. Therefore be alert and of sober mind so you can pray." I remember hearing a great sermon once where the preacher described this process as "clearing the decks." You have to clear your head of the junk top-of-mind; but you also have to keep it clear and not let it get foggy or clogged up. What things do you run to when you want to give your brain a break? TV, movies, social media, games, books? Too much consumption of this kind can make your mind go mushy and put you in danger of becoming slothful. The Amplified Version puts it well: "Therefore, be sound-minded and self-controlled for the purpose of prayer [staying balanced and focused on the things of God so that your communication will be clear, reasonable, specific and pleasing to Him.]"

What does the end of all things have to do with your prayer life? This quote, from the NIV Study Bible notes, clarified the connection to end times for me: "Anticipating end times, and in particular Christ's return, should influence believers' attitudes, actions, and relationships." Does your life reflect the influence of Christ's presence and His coming? How does His return influence your attitude, actions, and relationship to your husband? If you really believed our time was coming to an end, would you change? That question deserves some further consideration.

Peter goes on: "Above all, love each other deeply because love covers over a multitude of sins." More than any other relationship, this applies to you as a wife. A loving person forgives again and again. The Amplified Bible puts it this way: "have fervent and unfailing love." The Greek word translated "fervent" was used to describe the taut, stretched muscles of a runner winning the race. Forgiving love is a muscle exercised over and over in your marriage (and in the rest of life too). This kind of love "overlooks unkindness and unselfishly seeks the best for others" (AMP). Would anyone use these words to describe you?

Dallas Willard, in *Renovation of the Heart*, states: "To be self-obsessed, [is] to mistake one's own person for God," and "We should seriously inquire if to live in a world permeated with God and the knowledge of God is something we truly desire. If not, we can be assured that God will excuse us from His presence …. Wanting God to be God is very different from wanting God to help us."[7] Read that last sentence over again.

APPLICATION

What coping mechanisms do you run to in order to escape or to turn off your brain for a while?

Ask the Holy Spirit to reveal to you what needs to change. What will you need to do to stay self-controlled and alert?

Do you have forgiving love for your husband, a muscle that is stretched and exercised over and over?

Would people describe you as the one who overlooks unkindness and unselfishly seeks the best for the other person? Would your husband describe you this way?

---

7. Johnson and Willard, *Renovation of the Heart in Daily Practice*, 40–41.

Search your heart and answer honestly, Do you really desire a world permeated with God and the knowledge of God? Where do you resist?

Do you want God to be God, or do you really only want God to help you? Reflect on this and write a response to God.

#33 SELFLESS SERVING

1 Peter 4:9–11:
⁹ Offer hospitality to one another without grumbling. ¹⁰ Each of you should use whatever gift you have received to serve others, as faithful stewards of God's grace in its various forms. ¹¹ If anyone speaks, they should do so as one who speaks the very words of God. If anyone serves, they should do so with the strength God provides, so that in all things God may be praised through Jesus Christ. To him be the glory and the power for ever and ever. Amen.

FIRST PETER 4:9–11 is about hospitality and using your gifts to benefit others. "Hospitality ... without grumbling," it says. Usually, we think of hospitality in terms of serving or hosting others; can you apply these same principles to serving your husband? Do you look for ways to serve him in the same way you would serve important guests who were coming to stay at your home? This passage describes a selfless giving, such as throwing away all your plans in order to serve another person. Can you do that for your husband? For his friends you don't like? What is God expecting of you?

Do you apply this concept of "faithfully administering God's grace" to your service to others but avoid applying it to your home life? What do those words mean? How do you administer grace? The Amplified Version expands this way: "good stewards of God's multi-faceted grace [faithfully using the diverse, varied gifts and abilities granted to Christians by God's unmerited favour]." We normally think of this in terms of serving the body of Christ with our spiritual gifts; for example, if you have the gift of teaching, then you should be teaching others God's truths. I think sometimes we even can use this type of serving as an excuse to get away from our home life! However, we can also apply Peter's words to marriage. We are to be offering grace in every situation, in the church and in our home—the same grace God gives us.

How faithful are you in this? And when you speak, remember the intent of verse 11: using the very words of God and serving him in God's strength *so that God may be praised*. Note that He provides the words, and He provides the strength; our goal is to bring praise to Him.

I think that all of the excuses we might think up have just been wiped out.

APPLICATION

How hospitable are you? Do you like entertaining, helping people, serving others? Do you have the same response to your husband?

What can you do to be more hospitable to him?

What do the words "faithfully administering God's grace" mean?

How do you administer grace?

How faithful are you in this?

#34 YOUR CROSS

1 Peter 4:12–19:

¹² Dear friends, do not be surprised at the fiery ordeal that has come on you to test you, as though something strange were happening to you. ¹³ But rejoice inasmuch as you participate in the sufferings of Christ, so that you may be overjoyed when his glory is revealed. ¹⁴ If you are insulted because of the name of Christ, you are blessed, for the Spirit of glory and of God rests on you. ¹⁵ If you suffer, it should not be as a murderer or thief or any other kind of criminal, or even as a meddler. ¹⁶ However, if you suffer as a Christian, do not be ashamed, but praise God that you bear that name. ¹⁷ For it is time for judgment to begin with God's household; and if it begins with us, what will the outcome be for those who do not obey the gospel of God? ¹⁸ And,

"If it is hard for the righteous to be saved,

what will become of the ungodly and the sinner?"

¹⁹ So then, those who suffer according to God's will should commit themselves to their faithful Creator and continue to do good.

IN 1 PETER 4:12–14, Peter tells us that God purifies us through suffering. This whole passage is again about being insulted or persecuted for being a Christian. First of all, Peter says, "Do not be surprised ... as though something strange were happening." Instead, he says, "Rejoice!" You're participating in the sufferings of Christ. "If you are insulted because of the name of Christ, you are blessed, for the Spirit of glory and of God rests on you." Although your situation may be unique, suffering is universal. As Jesus told His disciples in Matthew 16:24, "Whoever wants to be my disciple must deny themselves and take up their cross and follow me." We are to follow in His steps, because He suffered for us. Your cross is yours alone. Spend time thinking about your cross and what it means. I don't think Jesus is talking about having a hangnail or putting up with an obnoxious co-worker.

Verse 15 points out that we can't blame God if we are suffering because we are sinful. Did you notice Peter puts meddling right up there with murder and stealing? Perhaps you know what it is like to suffer because you meddled in someone else's business. That's not God's fault.

However, don't be ashamed to suffer for being a Christian—"praise God that you bear that name." You're His child! It's an honour to bear His name; if you weren't His child, you wouldn't be suffering. Take comfort in that. Peter goes on to say it is time for judgment to begin with the family of God—Peter is pointing out that your suffering is necessary to cleanse you of your sin and purify you. If God's judgment begins with us, what will the outcome be for those who don't know God? If it's hard for the righteous to be saved, what will become of the ungodly?

"So then, those who suffer according to God's will should commit themselves to their faithful Creator and continue to do good." These are our action steps. Commit ourselves to God; continue to do good. And remember that those who don't know God will be judged; pray for them.

APPLICATION

Evaluate why you are suffering. Is it because of your own sin? Confess, repent, and turn away from that sin. Ask God to cleanse you and show you how to live in freedom from that sin.

Is your suffering not because of sin? Then trust God, and commit it to Him.

What is your cross? Ask God to clarify that for you; sometimes we call things a cross that are not at all.

Do you take it up daily? Remember His mercy is new every morning and you can pick that up too at the same time.

#35 TAKE OFF YOUR PROUD CLOTHING

1 Peter 5:1–7:

[1] To the elders among you, I appeal as a fellow elder and a witness of Christ's sufferings who also will share in the glory to be revealed: [2] Be shepherds of God's flock that is under your care, watching over them—not because you must, but because you are willing, as God wants you to be; not pursuing dishonest gain, but eager to serve; [3] not lording it over those entrusted to you, but being examples to the flock. [4] And when the Chief Shepherd appears, you will receive the crown of glory that will never fade away.

[5] In the same way, you who are younger, submit yourselves to your elders. All of you, clothe yourselves with humility towards one another, because,

"God opposes the proud
but shows favor to the humble."

[6] Humble yourselves, therefore, under God's mighty hand, that he may lift you up in due time. [7] Cast all your anxiety on him because he cares for you.

FIRST PETER 5:1–7 provides specific instructions to elders and overseers of the church (which may apply to you), but we will concentrate on our role as wives and not as church leaders. Peter also says, "All of you, clothe yourselves with humility toward one another." These verses talk about humility a lot. In a practical sense, how do you do that? Well, start by taking off your proud clothing: haughty eyes, superiority thinking, looking down on others, believing you're right.

"Be humble, thinking of others as better than yourself" (Philippians 2:3 NLT). *Serve* others. Listen instead of talking. Love deeply. Yield to the other person. Submit. "Humble yourselves, therefore, under God's mighty hand, that he may lift you up in due time." This is still related to experiencing suffering, false accusations, and insults because of Christ.

This may be a good time to review what you've written in your journal through our study and remember what the Lord taught you. I love what the Amplified Version states in verse 5-6: "[Tie on the servant's apron ... Set aside self-righteous pride]." This prayer from *The Valley of Vision* makes it personal: "Teach me to see ... that Christ does not desire me, now justified, to live in self-confidence in my own strength, but gives me the law of the Spirit of life to enable me to obey thee."[8] Yes, and amen.

When I was trying to crawl out of a hole I felt I was in, I once wrote out 1 Peter 5:5–7 as expressed in the Amplified Version by hand. The process cemented the text in my memory. Let me include it for you here:

All of you, clothe yourselves with humility toward one another [tie on the servant's apron], for God is opposed to the proud [the disdainful, the presumptuous, and He defeats them], but He gives grace to the humble.

Therefore humble yourselves under the mighty hand of God [set aside self-righteous pride] so that He may exalt you [to a place of honour in His service] at the appropriate time, casting all your cares [all your anxieties, all your worries, and all you concerns once and for all] on Him, for He cares about you [with deepest affection and watches over you very carefully].

APPLICATION

What "proud clothing" do you need to take off?

What clothing of humility do you need to put on in its place? Specifically, in what way can you tie on the servant's apron?

---

8. *The Valley of Vision*, 57.

Write out 1 Peter 5:5–7 by hand. Circle or underline any words or phrases that resonate with you.

What part of these verses resonates most deeply with you?

Do you feel yourself being humbled under God's hand? Or do you feel as if He's opposed to you in some way?

Look for those traits of pride or presumption or disdain, and see if they are operating in your life. In what ways do you need to cast your burdens on Him? My mentor used to tell me that she pictured herself throwing her burdens at God. I prefer to take them off my back, like heavy backpacks.

Allow the words "for He cares about you with deepest affection" to sink into your soul. Use these verses to create a prayer to God about how you're feeling, and recommit your trust in Him.

#36 OUR PROWLING ENEMY

1 Peter 5:8–9:
8 Be alert and of sober mind. Your enemy the devil prowls around like a roaring lion looking for someone to devour. 9 Resist him, standing firm in the faith, because you know that the family of believers throughout the world is undergoing the same kind of sufferings.

I HAVE A neighbor with an adult son who is mentally unstable and in and out of jail. He has broken into her home and assaulted her, trashed her furniture, stolen from her. Every time he gets out of jail, she takes precautions (changes the locks, obtains a restraining order, contacts the police and victim services), but she lives in constant fear that he's outside in the bushes, waiting to do her harm. What a terrible way to live!

It's not pleasant to think that we have an enemy who is prowling around. And we don't like to think about the forces of evil and spend our lives being fearful. I am sure God does not want us to be fearmongering; however, He does want us to be prepared. That's why 1 Peter 5:8 says, "Be sober [well-balanced and self-disciplined], be alert and cautious at all times. That enemy of yours, the devil, prowls around like a roaring lion [fiercely hungry], seeking someone to devour" (AMP).

As I was sorting through all of this in my own life, I once more saw myself standing at the bottom of a dark and foreboding mountain. "Not another mountain!" I cried, physically shaking with fear.

"One more," the Lord gently said.

But my apprehension held me back. "Lord, I want to be fearless." I find myself climbing already. I remember from 1 Peter 5, "Be alert and of sober mind, for your enemy the devil prowls around like a roaring lion looking for someone to devour." I feel like I would be easy pickings.

We have to be aware. God has warned us, and He is ready to protect us, but we can't be stupid about it. We are to be sober-minded, alert, and cautious. We know Satan is lurking and we have to be on guard. He doesn't have a foothold in our life if we don't give him one. But our sinful attitudes, our unresolved anger, our bitterness and resentment, even our lack of love can all give him a way to get in. We need to be bulletproof.

God tells us what to do: "resist him, be firm in your faith [against his attack—rooted, established, immovable], knowing that the same experiences of suffering are being experienced by your brothers and sisters throughout the world. [You do not suffer alone.]" (AMP). When Satan tempts you to discouragement or despair, resist him! Search your heart and confess whatever may be there; take back any footholds given to the enemy, in the name of Jesus. Then stand firm; remember that the enemy has no jurisdiction in your life, marriage, or home. And take courage in the knowledge that you are not alone—the same experiences of suffering for the Lord are going on all over the world.

The enemy is prowling to bring you down, zeroing in on your new resolve, your changed heart. God is not telling you this to give you a new fear; it is a warning not to relax and get complacent again.

In *Renovation of the Heart*, Dallas Willard gives an adaptation of Psalm 23. "In those dramatic moments when I face those who oppose me, dislike me or just plain annoy me, I find God behind me, pouring love into me, giving me just what I need. Actually, what I need overflows!"[9]

APPLICATION

Are you facing another mountain? What is the mountain? Take Jesus's hand as you journey forward together.

---

9. Johnson and Willard, *Renovation of the Heart in Daily Practice*, 50.

Find safety verses in Scripture, and memorize them; choose ones that apply directly to your situation. I like Psalm 27:5: "He will conceal me ... when troubles come. He will hide me in His sanctuary. He will place me out of reach on a high rock" (NLT). God hides you. Visualize that high rock; look down on your enemies. Thank Him for concealing you.

Give some thought to "resisting the devil." You need to be prepared for it: temptation, attacks, opposition. By being alert, you'll see the tactics of the enemy coming; by being self-controlled, you won't be walking into the enemy's traps deliberately. Remember, neither your husband nor any other human is the enemy. Satan is. Fear is. Stand firm in faith—not running to hide, not giving in to doubt. You are not alone; there are many others.

#37 A PROMISE AND A BLESSING

1 Peter 5:10–12:
[10] And the God of all grace, who called you to his eternal glory in Christ, after you have suffered a little while, will himself restore you and make you strong, firm and steadfast. [11] To him be the power for ever and ever. Amen.

[12] With the help of Silas, whom I regard as a faithful brother, I have written to you briefly, encouraging you and testifying that this is the true grace of God. Stand fast in it.

A promise and a blessing: "After you have suffered a little while, the God of all grace [who imparts His blessing and favour], who called you to His own eternal glory in Christ, will Himself complete, confirm, strengthen, and establish you [making you what you ought to be]" (AMP).

There's the theme of "called" again. It seems like we are called to lots of things in 1 Peter. The Lord called you to His own glory. What does that mean? Has He called you to Himself? To share His glory in eternity? Just let your mind try to wrap about that calling for a few moments.

Let's break down the four promises from verse 10:

Complete. God's promise is that He will Himself complete you, as in Philippians 1:6. He began the good work in you, and He will bring it to completion.

Confirm. What you have done and are doing is His will, is right, is best.

Strengthen. God will renew your spiritual, emotional, and physical strength.

Establish. God has set you in place, on a firm foundation, settled in a location with purpose, built up over time like establishing a business that thrives—just as if you're getting established in your community or in your church.

We are almost done in 1 Peter, and he ends his letter with the encouragement of verses 10 and 12; "In His kindness God called you to share in his eternal glory by means of Christ Jesus. So after you have suffered a little while, he will restore, support, and strengthen you, and he will place you on a firm foundation ... My purpose in writing is to encourage you and assure you that what you are experiencing is truly part of God's grace for you. Stand firm in this grace" (NLT). This is God's grace for you. Ask God to help you to see what He is talking about.

In *Renovation of the Heart*, Dallas Willard comments on self-denial: "To accept with confidence in God that we do not have to get our own way releases us from the great pressure that anger, unforgiveness and the 'need' to retaliate impose upon our lives."[10]

APPLICATION

What do you think it means that God called you to His glory? How can you apply that truth to yourself?

Take the four promises and apply them to your own life. Are there any Scriptures that come to mind that are meaningful for you? Here are some of my favorites:

Complete: "being confident of this, that he who began a good work in you will carry it on to completion until the day of Christ Jesus" (Philippians 1:6).

Confirm: "He will make your righteous reward shine like the dawn, your vindication like the noonday sun" (Psalm 37:6).

Strengthen: "but those who hope in the Lord will renew their strength. They will soar on wings like eagles; they will run and not grow weary, they will walk and not be faint" (Isaiah 40:31).

Establish: "I said, 'You are my servant'; I have chosen you and have not rejected you. So do not fear, for I am with you; do not be dismayed, for I am your God. I will strengthen you and help you; I will uphold you with my righteous right hand" (Isaiah 41:9–10).

---

10. Johnson and Willard, *Renovation of the Heart in Daily Practice*, 52.

What Scriptures give you encouragement and reminders in each of these four areas? Apply those to your own life, and write a prayer to the Lord for each one. Copy down the Scriptures, and carry them with you for the next week, as a reminder.

In Mark, James and John ask Jesus to do for them whatever they ask. What would you ask?

Pray the prayer from *Renovation of the Heart*, and ask God to make it true of your life. "To accept with confidence in God that we do not have to get our own way releases us from the great pressure that anger, unforgiveness and the 'need' to retaliate impose upon our lives."

Part 2

FREEDOM FROM UNFORGIVENSS, ANGER, FEAR

FREEDOM THROUGH FORGIVENESS[11]

11. I am deeply indebted to David Chotka for his book, *Power Praying* (Terre Haute: Prayer Shop Publishing, 2009), which impacted my prayer life especially in the area of forgiveness. His concepts have shaped my understanding of what it means to truly forgive.

#1 WHY DO I HAVE TO FORGIVE?

THE PREMISE FOR this study on forgiveness is the line from the Lord's prayer: "Forgive us our debts, as we have also forgiven our debtors" (Matthew 6:12).

As a Christian, you know you are forgiven. God has forgiven you for all your sins through His death on the cross. It is the basis of your new life. So you start with being forgiven by God for all your sin; but then you must live out that forgiveness by forgiving those who sin against you. This is not always easy, especially with those who are closest to us (like our husbands).

This is also the message of the Parable of the Prodigal Son (see Luke 15:11–32) and its connection to family members. Often, we read this parable and place ourselves in the person of the prodigal as someone who needs to come to God in repentance. But we can also relate to the older brother. We need to realize that when we withhold forgiveness, we are acting like the older brother. What qualities do you see in him? He was judgmental, unforgiving, unrepentant, self-righteous, and quick to blame the father. The message is clear: we who are forgiven need to be ready to forgive others even when we feel they don't deserve it.

God has called you to be a forgiving person, and God strongly warns of consequences for those who do not forgive. Matthew 6:12 says, "forgive us our debts, as we have forgiven our debtors [letting go of both the wrong and the resentment]" (AMP). Jesus does not stop there. Do you know what the verse following the Lord's Prayer says? "For if you forgive others their trespasses [their reckless and willful sins], your heavenly Father will also forgive you. But if you do not forgive others [nurturing your hurt and anger with the result that it interferes with your relationship with God], then your Father will not forgive your trespasses" (verses 14–15 AMP). Is God lying or telling the truth? Jesus says the Father *will not* forgive; this is sobering.

Forgiveness is a choice. It is refusing to be bound by yesterday's transgressions—yours or another's. Let's be sure to work through this important need to forgive.

APPLICATION

Read Luke 15:11–32: The Parable of the Prodigal Son

[11] Jesus continued: "There was a man who had two sons. [12] The younger one said to his father, 'Father, give me my share of the estate.' So he divided his property between them.

[13] "Not long after that, the younger son got together all he had, set off for a distant country and there squandered his wealth in wild living. [14] After he had spent everything, there was a severe famine in that whole country, and he began to be in need. [15] So he went and hired himself out to a citizen of that country, who sent him to his fields to feed pigs. [16] He longed to fill his stomach with the pods that the pigs were eating, but no one gave him anything.

[17] "When he came to his senses, he said, 'How many of my father's hired servants have food to spare, and here I am starving to death! [18] I will set out and go back to my father and say to him: Father, I have sinned against heaven and against you. [19] I am no longer worthy to be called your son; make me like one of your hired servants.' [20] So he got up and went to his father.

"But while he was still a long way off, his father saw him and was filled with compassion for him; he ran to his son, threw his arms around him and kissed him.

[21] "The son said to him, 'Father, I have sinned against heaven and against you. I am no longer worthy to be called your son.'

[22] "But the father said to his servants, 'Quick! Bring the best robe and put it on him. Put a ring on his finger and sandals on his feet. [23] Bring the fattened calf and kill it. Let's have a feast and celebrate. [24] For this son of mine was dead and is alive again; he was lost and is found.' So they began to celebrate.

[25] "Meanwhile, the elder son was in the field. When he came near the house, he heard music and dancing. [26] So he called one of the servants and asked him what was going on. [27] 'Your brother has come,' he replied, 'and your father has killed the fattened calf because he has him back safe and sound.'

[28] "The older brother became angry and refused to go in. So his father went out and pleaded with him. [29] But he answered

his father, 'Look! All these years I've been slaving for you and never disobeyed your orders. Yet you never gave me even a young goat so I could celebrate with my friends. [30] But when this son of yours who has squandered your property with prostitutes comes home, you kill the fattened calf for him!'

[31] "'My son,' the father said, 'you are always with me, and everything I have is yours. [32] But we had to celebrate and be glad, because this brother of yours was dead and is alive again; he was lost and is found.'"

Read over the parable slowly, three times. Place yourself in the story first as the prodigal; next as the loving father, and finally as the older brother. Write down whatever the Lord brings to mind. Take a good amount of time to do this.

When you reflect on the older brother, what qualities do you see in him? Do you have any of these qualities? Take some time to talk about this with the Lord. Write down what He brings to mind.

Read again Matthew 6:14–15. "If you forgive other people when they sin against you, your heavenly Father will also forgive you. But if you do not forgive others their sins, your Father will not forgive your sins." What are the consequences of not forgiving?

Do you think God is telling the truth?

#2 BITTER ROOT

Matthew 18:21–35:

²¹ Then Peter came to Jesus and asked, "Lord, how many times shall I forgive my brother or sister who sins against me? Up to seven times?"

²² Jesus answered, "I tell you, not seven times, but seventy-seven times.

²³ "Therefore, the kingdom of heaven is like a king who wanted to settle accounts with his servants. ²⁴ As he began the settlement, a man who owed him ten thousand bags of gold was brought to him. ²⁵ Since he was not able to pay, the master ordered that he and his wife and his children and all that he had be sold to repay the debt.

²⁶ "At this the servant fell on his knees before him. 'Be patient with me,' he begged, 'and I will pay back everything.' ²⁷ The servant's master took pity on him, canceled the debt and let him go.

²⁸ "But when that servant went out, he found one of his fellow servants who owed him a hundred silver coins. He grabbed him and began to choke him. 'Pay back what you owe me!' he demanded.

²⁹ "His fellow servant fell to his knees and begged him, 'Be patient with me, and I will pay it back.'

³⁰ "But he refused. Instead, he went off and had the man thrown into prison until he could pay the debt. ³¹ When the other servants saw what had happened, they were outraged and went and told their master everything that had happened.

³² "Then the master called the servant in. 'You wicked servant,' he said, 'I cancelled all that debt of yours because you begged me to. ³³ Shouldn't you have had mercy on your fellow servant just as I had on you?' ³⁴ In anger his master handed him over to the jailers to be tortured, until he should pay back all he owed.

³⁵ "This is how my heavenly Father will treat each of you unless you forgive your brother or sister from your heart."

FORGIVENESS IS A choice. An act of your will, not based on feelings. When you don't forgive, you are in bondage to the actions of the past, whether yours or another's.

Hebrews 12:14–15 lays out God's expectation of us: "Work at living in peace with everyone, and work at living a holy life, for those who are not holy will not see the Lord. Look after each other so that none of you fails to receive the grace of God. Watch out that no poisonous root of bitterness grows up to trouble you, corrupting many" (NLT).

Resentment and bitterness are poisonous roots that grow when forgiveness is withheld from the person who offended you. "Bitterness is nothing more than old unforgiveness."[12] Jesus is telling you not only to forgive but also to pray for your own forgiveness based on how you extend it to others. Your goal should be to deal with offenses quickly and stop keeping score.

Jesus spoke more than once about the need to forgive. Note that the Lord's prayer says "Forgive our debts as we forgive" (meaning, in the same way we forgive). Do you forgive fully from your heart? Is your forgiveness sacrificial or superficial? There's a good test for this: How much emotion do you feel when you think about the person or the incident? Are you still carrying around anger or resentment that bubbles up to the surface the minute you are reminded?

In Matthew 18, the Parable of the Unforgiving Servant concludes by saying the master "handed him over to the jailers to be tortured … this is how my heavenly Father will treat each of you unless you forgive your brother or sister from your heart." What are the jailers torturing you? Here are a few that I can think of:

- nagging guilt
- painful memories/reminders
- regret, defeat, despair
- physical ailments, including stomach aches, tension, headaches
- cynicism and a critical attitude
- hardness and coldness toward others
- anger, hurt, feelings of betrayal
- spiritual attacks

---

12. Chotka, *Power Praying*, 189.

Along with the person you won't forgive, your relationship with everyone will be affected if you are experiencing any of these things. If you find yourself being tortured in any of these ways, take heart! God wants you to walk in freedom, and He has provided a way for you to be free.

APPLICATION

Have you tried to forgive someone, but suddenly you're blindsided by anger or emotion when a memory is triggered?

How do you know if you have truly forgiven that person?

Here are some questions to ask yourself as you work through fully forgiving the offense:

- Do you see the person coming and have the impulse to turn and walk the other way?
- If you see the person's car in the parking lot, do you want to avoid going into the same location?
- Do you expect the person to do something bad to you instead of good?
- Do you run through scenarios in your mind of confrontations, always thinking how you will shut them down or get back at them?
- Do you plan out your conversations because you want to be prepared for their arguments, thereby deciding ahead of time what they will say or do?

If so, then you are still holding something against them, and true forgiveness is needed. Ask the Lord to show you if there is any other unforgiveness you haven't dealt with.

Before you move on and read the third study on forgiveness, ask the Lord to prepare your heart to want to forgive.

#3 EXPERIENCING TRUE FORGIVENESS

IN THE BOOK *Power Praying*, author David Chotka gives us these four steps to outline what true forgiveness is:[13]

- Acknowledging someone has ruined your life.
- Declaring to God (and to them if possible) that you will neither seek retribution nor treat them as their sins deserve.
- Choosing to let them off your hook for God to do with them as He sees fit (put them on His hook).
- Praying a blessing on them, as Christ commanded.

APPLICATION

Who are the people in your life who have hurt you?

Do painful experiences still come back to haunt you with anger? Do you still feel emotion when you think of what happened? Those are indications that true forgiveness is not yet complete. If this is the case, make a plan to forgive.

You need an action plan. I'm grateful to David Chotka, who provided this list in his book *Power Praying*. He suggests this outline:[14]

---

13. Chotka, *Power Praying*, 194.
14. Chotka, *Power Praying*, 195.

Review the four steps of forgiveness, then:

- Take one of the memories, and name the fact that the person, group, or situation truly did injure you, and you paid for it.
- Declare to the Lord that you will absorb their sin (this is what forgiveness does) and bear the cost of their injuring you.
- Picture the cross of Christ. Deliberately place this pain-memory on it, and tell the Lord you will not pick it up again. (Anytime the memory returns, return to this picture of the sin against you dead on the cross.)
- Choose to pray a blessing that will make the person who sinned against you more like Christ. (If people stole from you, pray they would receive generosity. If they lied, pray that they become utterly truthful. If they manipulated a situation at your expense, pray that they become forthright and fair.) Bless them with this prayer every time you remember them and ask God to fill them with His presence.
- Close your prayer with thanksgiving that God has had mercy on us and saved us for Himself.

PRAYER CHALLENGE:

This kind of praying can lead to many memories of past injustices. Each time one of these comes to mind, jot it down so that you can take it to the cross when you are able. Then praise God that He is calling you to wholeness. Deliberately thank Him. Use a psalm or sing a praise song with each memory. God is healing your soul. Thank Him.

#4 AVOIDANCE

IT MAKES SENSE to take a closer look at the ways we avoid forgiving. These may not even be conscious actions on your part. Maybe you absorb or bury the hurt because it can be just too painful to deal with. If so, then you need to know that "stuffing it" is not forgiving. If you bury it in this way, you are only fostering it, and it will grow worse.

By burying the hurt and pain of the past, you allow a bitter root to grow in your heart. Later, it is much more work to get rid of. Just as in your garden, pulling a weed when it breaks the surface is easy because the root is shallow and weak. However, if you wait until the weed is four feet high, you will have a much harder time; when you pull it, you will realize the root has become a tap root, long and thick and unwilling to give up its hold on the soil.

The alternative is to choose to forgive and ask God to redeem or buy back the injury. Walk through the situation with Jesus, and let Him heal. When you think you can't forgive on your own, God can do it through you.

When Corrie ten Boom, who spent time in a Nazi prison camp for hiding Jews, faced one of her prison guards, she found she could not forgive. She asked the Lord, "Give me Your forgiveness" and as she reached out to shake the hand of the guard, she felt a current pass through her arm to his hand, and love came in and filled her. God wants to fill you with His forgiveness when you can't forgive on your own. Or when you think you have forgiven fully but you find the bitterness remains. What it requires is a decision.

APPLICATION

Are there any old incidents you have stuffed?

Have they been growing in you like that weed, and now the root is deep in your heart? You need to release it to the Lord. God takes what is awful, ugly, broken, or painful and turns it into something beautiful. Make a list of the things you have stuffed down and remain there, that have not been dealt with.

Corrie ten Boom said: "It's not on our forgiveness any more than on our goodness that the world's healing hinges, but on His. When He tells us to love our enemies, He gives, along with the command, the love itself."[15] Forgiveness isn't going to happen just because you say in your head, "Okay, I forgive so-and-so." How often do you think you've forgiven someone, and yet the old offense comes right back to your mind as soon as the person does the same thing again? That's a good sign you haven't forgiven. Ask the Lord for power to forgive your list of offenses against another person. You can't do it yourself. Go through David Chotka's four steps in Forgiveness #3 for each event, and ask God to turn them into something beautiful. Thank Him for His grace and for power to transform you into His image. End your time by praising Him.

---

15. Chotka, *Power Praying*, 200.

#5 FORGIVING IS NOT FORGETTING

THERE IS AN account of Pastor Lang, whose son was shot in the high school in Taber, Alberta. The day following the shooting, he stood on the exact spot where his son was gunned down and called people back in the name of the Lord. He forgave—but he can't forget what happened. He won't ever forget his son; nor will he ever forget the way he died.

Biblical sins were forgiven by God and the situations redeemed (such as the sin of David with Bathsheba and Uriah in 2 Samuel 11–12), but God recorded them forever in His Word. To forgive is not to forget. It's not even to trust. For example, suppose you had an employee who stole from the cash register and was caught. You can forgive, not press charges, not ask for restitution, and cover the loss yourself; you can let the person keep their job and not bring it up anymore or discipline them; but you don't put them immediately back in control of the cash! It is likely you cannot forget; but you can get to the place where you choose to accept that someone ruined your life. You can pay the cost yourself, as Christ did, trusting God to redeem your losses in some way.

In His Word, God says He "remembers your sins no more" (Isaiah 43:25), but that doesn't mean He forgets them; nor does He always remove the consequences. Forgetting is a flaw and God is perfect and omniscient. He *chooses* not to use the past against us.

Just as with our Father, forgiveness is a choice, a crisis of will. Maybe you don't want to let your husband off the hook. If that's the case, it's *you* who are *still hooked* yourself. He hurt you in the past and by your not forgiving him, he still is hurting you! If not for his sake, forgive him for yours.

Forgiveness is agreeing to live with the consequences of another person's sin. You are going to live with the consequences anyway; the question is, will you live in bitterness or freedom? Just as Jesus was made sin for us, true forgiveness is substitutionary.

How do you forgive from your heart?

Acknowledge the hurt and hate. Accept responsibility for your part in the incident. Let God bring the pain to the surface. *Decide* to bear the burden of the offense by not using the information in the future. Don't wait until you feel like it—you won't. The feeling will come after the healing. Freedom, not feeling, is gained.

APPLICATION

Find an hour to spend alone. Take some time praising God, settle into His presence, and ask Him to bring to mind people you need to forgive. Write their names down and follow this outline for each one: "Lord, I forgive _____ for _____.
I take them off my hook and trust them to Yours for whatever will bring grace to their lives. Redeem their lives, even as I trust You to redeem what I have lost through their sin."

FREEDOM FROM ANGER

#1 THE ANNOYANCES BUZZING AROUND US[16]

DO YOU EVER go camping? It's one of the things our family enjoys very much. If you do, you have probably had the experience of getting into a sleeping bag and realizing there's a mosquito in the tent with you. And once you realize it, there is no way you can sleep until you do everything you can to get rid of it.

What is buzzing around in your life like that annoying mosquito? What have you been doing about it? Often, we become hurt, bitter, and angry because of the actions of another person, and we clutch on to it, rehearsing it over and over in our minds, letting it continue to hurt and cause us pain.

Is living with bitterness better than putting in the work to restore a relationship?

Is living with hurt and brokenness better than putting in the work to restore a relationship?

Why don't we work as hard to get rid of those things in our heart as we do the mosquito in our tent?

Let's take a look at Ephesians 4, where Paul talks about how we should act as Christians. He starts off this section in 4:1, "I beg you to live a life worthy of your calling" (NLT). Let your mind go back to your calling; what has God called you to? Even if there's nothing more you can think of than being His child, that's enough. How do you live a life worthy of all God has called you to?

Paul also talks about anger: "Don't sin by letting anger control you" (Ephesians 4:26). The Amplified Version says "Be angry, yet do not sin". Stop there for a moment. It actually says, "Be angry." Yes. Anger is not a sin, it's an emotion or reaction. How you deal with it is where sin can come in.

Paul continues in verse 26: "Don't let the sun go down while you're still angry." Don't hold on to it—it will control you—*this* is sin. How do you keep from sinning in anger?

---

16. I am grateful to Rev. David Brotherton for the outline of this study, preached at Sauble Christian Fellowship in the summer of 2019 as a part of a series on the Seven Deadly Sins. Used with permission.

- Don't hold on to it.
- Don't sin by letting anger control you.
- Don't let it linger (past sundown).
- Clear it!

There's a quote from the comedienne Phyllis Diller, "Don't go to bed while you're still angry; stay up and fight!" Maybe not the best way of dealing with our anger, but she has a point. When we allow anger to remain, it simmers; it just doesn't fade away when you squash it. When we don't deal with it, it overpowers the heart. That's why God commanded us not to let the sun go down while we are still angry (see Ephesians 4:26).

APPLICATION

Think through your answers to the questions: Is living with bitterness better than putting in the work to restore a relationship? Is living with hurt and brokenness better than putting in the work to restore a relationship?

Why don't we work as hard to get rid of those things as we do the mosquito?

Why have you been holding on to anger?

What have you been learning in our study so far to help you live a worthy life of God's calling on your life?

In what ways have you been letting anger control you?

Review these steps and think of how you can put them into action to help you keep from sinning in anger.

- Don't hold on to it.
- Don't sin by letting anger control you.
- Don't let it linger (past sundown).
- *Clear it!*

#2 THE CONSEQUENCES OF HOLDING ON TO ANGER

ANGER ISN'T SIN, it's an emotion or reaction. But holding on to it is a *decision*. It's how we respond or deal with anger that can lead us to sin. Ephesians 4:27 says, "Anger gives a foothold to the devil" (NLT). When we are angry, we are offering Satan a gift. Pastor Brotherton explains, "Anger *gives* (gifts, supplies, commits) a foothold (staging area, literally) to the devil." You're giving an open invitation to set up shop in your life. Is that what you want? I'm sure it isn't. And yet this is what happens when we let anger linger.

As well, there's a consequence in your relationship with God. Ephesians 4:30 says, "Do not bring sorrow to God's Holy Spirit by the way you live" (NLT). God has already set you free, but you're choosing to sit in your prison cell, where Satan holds you captive through your unforgiveness and anger. And verse 31 continues, "get rid of all bitterness, rage, anger, harsh words, and slander" (NLT). Note that the passage doesn't talk about what the other person has done; this is all about you and your reactions and responses to them.

What do you do instead? Ephesians 4:32 gives us the answer: "Be kind to each other, tenderhearted, forgiving one another" (NLT). In the Greek, the word translated "forgive" indicates a full pardon. What does it mean to offer a full pardon? It means you have to cancel the debt you feel they owe you; the only way to get rid of the anger is to forgive. This is more than just saying, "I forgive you"; it is full, unconditional forgiveness. Verse 32 continues, "just as God through Christ has forgiven you" (NLT). You must forgive in the same way that God has done it for you: He gives you undeserved grace, and He chooses to let you go free. If He has done this for you, how dare you hold someone else hostage?

How do you find freedom from your anger? Here are four things you can do:

- Identify and face the truth about your anger (see Psalm 139:23–24).
- Choose to cancel the debt.

- Courageously ask for forgiveness for holding on to it (ask the other person), even if the relationship isn't repaired.
- Rely on God's strength. Every time God asks us to do something big, He says "I will be with you."

First Peter 4:19 states: "So if you find life difficult because you're doing what God said, take it in stride. Trust Him. He knows what He's doing, and He'll keep on doing it" (MSG).

APPLICATION

Read the Parable of the Unjust Servant in Matthew 18:21–35.

²¹ Then Peter came to Jesus and asked, "Lord, how many times shall I forgive my brother or sister who sins against me? Up to seven times?"

²² Jesus answered, "I tell you, not seven times, but seventy-seven times.

²³ "Therefore, the kingdom of heaven is like a king who wanted to settle accounts with his servants. ²⁴ As he began the settlement, a man who owed him ten thousand bags of gold was brought to him. ²⁵ Since he was not able to pay, the master ordered that he and his wife and his children and all that he had be sold to repay the debt.

²⁶ "At this the servant fell on his knees before him. 'Be patient with me,' he begged, 'and I will pay back everything.' ²⁷ The servant's master took pity on him, canceled the debt and let him go.

²⁸ "But when that servant went out, he found one of his fellow servants who owed him a hundred silver coins. He grabbed him and began to choke him. 'Pay back what you owe me!' he demanded.

²⁹ "His fellow servant fell to his knees and begged him, 'Be patient with me, and I will pay it back.'

³⁰ "But he refused. Instead, he went off and had the man thrown into prison until he could pay the debt. ³¹ When the other servants saw what had happened, they were outraged

and went and told their master everything that had happened.

³² "Then the master called the servant in. 'You wicked servant,' he said, 'I cancelled all that debt of yours because you
begged me to. ³³ Shouldn't you have had mercy on your fellow
servant just as I had on you?' ³⁴ In anger his master handed him over to the jailers to be tortured, until he should pay
back all he owed.

³⁵ "This is how my heavenly Father will treat each of you
unless you forgive your brother or sister from your heart."

The king represents God, who has freely forgiven your enormous
debt of sin. Ten thousand talents would be millions of dollars in today's economy. Spend some time contemplating your debt, which
has been forgiven. God cancelled the debt! You owe nothing; you
walk away free.

Now put yourself in the place of the unmerciful servant. This is what
your anger has done. Comparatively, the person owes you only a few
dollars. Whom have you held captive because of your anger and unforgiveness? If God has done this for you, how dare you hold someone else hostage?

Go through the steps to freedom, and ask the Holy Spirit to lead you.
Write down whatever He has prompted you to do. Don't delay.

FREEDOM FROM FEAR

#1 THE PIT AND THE GIANT

I HAD A dream the other night. In my dream, I was completely in the dark. I waited for my eyes to adjust, but I could still see nothing at all. I stretched out my hands and felt around me—it felt like a damp, clammy stone wall; a circle like a well and the wall lined with stones or bricks. Above me also was dark; I didn't know how high the ceiling was or what was up there. I only knew I couldn't see anything but darkness.

It seems odd now that I don't remember feeling afraid. I just tried to figure out what to do. I reached up the wall and found a hand-hold. I dug into the stones with my foot until I found a toehold, and I started to climb. It was very slippery, and I slid down many times. I climbed higher and higher, sliding back down and having to start over more times than I could count. Eventually, my perseverance paid off, and my hand hit something hard above me. I pushed on it (as well as I could with one hand), but it wouldn't budge. I tried to slide it over, and it moved slightly; it appeared to be dark on the other side as well. Then I woke up.

It didn't take me long to figure out that my pit represented fear. It has a grip on me still, and I wonder if my dream and my experience of trying to climb out represents my own efforts in battling my fears. Rather than looking to God, I charge ahead with a kind of spiritual self-help mentality and realize later I'm doing everything in my own strength. It's not working, so I petition the Lord to show me what He wants from me.

One thing I know is that I focus too much on myself and not enough on Him. I remember from years ago hearing a sermon that talked about the Goliath in our lives. What is the giant that is staring you down, taunting you, holding you back? Fear is definitely that for me right now. The pastor suggested that just as David grabbed five smooth stones from the brook to defeat Goliath, I need to find five smooth stones of Scripture to hurl at the enemy whenever I am faced with that Goliath in my own life. I've used this concept for many temptations and found it very helpful. What were five smooth stones for me in this instance? What verses could I write down and memorize to pull out when I felt fearful?

Seek the Lord for five key verses to use against the enemy. Two of my favourites: "The Spirit you received does not make you slaves, so that you live in fear again; rather, the Spirit you received brought about your adoption to sonship" (Romans 8:15) and "For God has not given us a spirit of fear and timidity, but of power, love, and self-discipline" (2 Timothy 1:7 NLT).

APPLICATION

What image comes to mind when you think of your fear? How does it make you feel?

Have you been trying to combat your fear in your own strength? In what ways?

What are the Goliaths in your life? Spend some time talking to God about this, and let Him reveal what He sees in you. It may not be what you think.

What are five smooth stones of Scripture you can put in your arsenal to combat the giant when he is lurking?

Over the next few days, ask God to bring to mind Scripture verses you can use for this purpose. Write them down and carry them with you; post them on your computer screen, make them your background on your phone. Use them as you need to, and do your best to memorize them. Ask the Holy Spirit to bring them to mind whenever fear comes calling.

#2 WHAT IS BEHIND YOUR FEAR?

I HAVE OFTEN battled fear. When I have discussed my fear with my spiritual mentor, she has poked and prodded, asking me what I was afraid of and trying to get below the surface. Usually, it helps for a while, but then a new fear emerges or old ones resurface, seemingly more powerful than ever. Scripture tells us many times, "Do not fear." I go through a cycle of confessing over and over, but fear always comes back. Ultimately, rather than trusting God, I am allowing my fears to invade like an army because of my doubt.

Recently, my mentor told me something that was a complete paradigm shift for me. She told me that fear was an emotion, and the purpose of an emotion is to tell us about ourselves and to reveal what we value. It took me a while to let this sink in: My fear is only alerting me to what is going on and what I need to release to God. This was revolutionary!

Once I started to think about the things I feared, it didn't take me too long to realize that I had one big fear that seemed, like Goliath, to lead the rest of the army of fears invading my mind daily. God showed me that I didn't want my husband to have control over my life with his excessive drinking or use of drugs or bad decisions or wasteful spending; I thought I needed to take control of the things I could so that his control wouldn't adversely affect me. Of course, ultimately this meant I wasn't letting God have control. Somehow, I had convinced myself that God wasn't going to protect me, so I had to do it myself. Sometimes I think that my control of our finances, home, and activities, and even filtering the information I give my husband, is okay with God. But I realized that I had control issues; it was deep, and it was ugly.

That day, I gave control of my life over to God. Every bit of it. I had done this many times before; but this time was different. I had to decide: do I trust God or not? If my husband is out of control, that's God's business; this fear is not mine to carry. The Lord was telling me to *let go*, and I did. I asked Him for the grace to sustain me when fears come creeping back.

I cannot begin to describe the peace that invaded my life that day. I've been a Christian for more than fifty years, and I have not ever experienced anything close to this. And believe me, my life has not been a bed of roses since then. Actually, the opposite is true. Accidents, injury, and illness all happened within a couple of days; including the most extreme drunken episode I have ever experienced with my husband. Scary stuff—but I was not scared or stressed or fearful. God was holding me, and this time I *knew* it was true.

APPLICATION

First of all, sit with the thought that your fear is an emotion, telling you something about yourself. Let this sink in. Ask God to reveal the truth of this to you, so that you are convinced. Next, sift through the layers of your fears to get to the root fear. Ask the Holy Spirit to guide your mind as you examine your life.

Write down what you find that gives you fear, and ask God, "Is there something deeper?" Don't rush this; take your time. It may take a few days.

I find it helpful to answer the question "*What* am I afraid of?" out loud. Then ask, "*Why* am I afraid of that?" Keep going, speaking each new fear that arises, until you get to the root. You may find that as you go deeper, it gets harder to speak it out loud.

As you go through those things, lift them up to God, and ask Him to heal and cleanse where these are needed. I suspect the deeper you go, the harder it will be to acknowledge and release your fear-motivator to God. There may be something you have to deal with, something that you should have done a long time ago. Ask God to increase your faith and to let you feel His presence with you as you release it all to Him.

Finally, ask Him to give you His peace. If it is helpful, breathe out the thing that is making you fear, and breathe in the Spirit of peace.

#3 WHAT IF FEAR WON'T STAY AWAY?

AS WE WORK to overcome fear, what do we need to keep in mind? We need to be on the alert for indications that our fear is returning. It's great to rest in the freedom God has given us and soak in His peace, but don't fool yourself into thinking that a test isn't coming. You may be acutely aware of the big sin that is causing your fear, but what about the smaller sins that are by-products of that fear? Things like worry, or lying, or silent slander?

Worry is something that all of us deal with and is one issue that some Christians don't seem to take very seriously. I read recently that worry is nothing more than believing God is about to get it wrong. Would you ever consciously think that? Probably not—yet we worry about the future, money, and our families *all the time.*

In the Sermon on the Mount, Jesus tells us not to worry about our life (see Matthew 6:25–34). Don't allow yourself to be lulled into thinking it's not important or you can't help it. Trusting Him is extremely important, and if you are worrying, you are not trusting.

How much of your fear is closely aligned with your worries? When you indulge in worry and it causes you to fear, it's as if you are telling God that you believe His intent is to leave you unprotected and vulnerable. Read that again. Do you believe God intends to leave you unprotected? Or vulnerable? Do you think He just lets bad things happen or that your life is beyond His control? Think over your answer carefully.

I know it's not enough to say, "Worry be gone!" You must confess and repent, but you also must *replace* your worry with something positive. During a time when my husband's mismanagement of our business caused us to lose everything—home, business, savings—I knew I had to take action against the worries and fears that bombarded me on every side. So I asked the Holy Spirit to bring a song to mind every time my thoughts turned to my troubles. It worked! God was so faithful, and I felt Him so near. The lawyers I worked with used to laugh that I was always humming; but they also noticed that although my life was falling apart around me, my trust in God kept me at peace. This is a testimony without words—and this peace is what God wants for all of His children. Even you.

What will it take for you to trust God enough that all of your worries disappear?

APPLICATION

What are the sins in your life that tag along behind your fear? Give some thought to this, and write them down.

Are there sins you just ignore or don't think of as important? Talk to God about this.

Where has worry taken over in your life? Are you wrapped up in anxiety?

Are you ready to confess and repent? To repent means to change your old way of thinking, turn from your sinful ways, and live a changed life. Take some time to think through all those steps.

What can you replace your worry with? Talk with the Lord about this, and follow His lead. Commit your way forward to Him. Ask Him, "Where is the path to peace?"

Part 3

2 PETER

GROWING

#1 KEEP FROM BEING INEFFECTIVE AND UNPRODUCTIVE

2 Peter 1:3–9:

³ His divine power has given us everything we need for a godly life through our knowledge of him who called us by his own glory and goodness. ⁴ Through these he has given us his very great and precious promises, so that through them you may participate in the divine nature, having escaped the corruption in the world caused by evil desires.

⁵ For this very reason, make every effort to add to your faith goodness; and to goodness, knowledge; ⁶ and to knowledge, self-control; and to self-control, perseverance; and to perseverance, godliness; ⁷ and to godliness, mutual affection; and to mutual affection, love. ⁸ For if you possess these qualities in increasing measure, they will keep you from being ineffective and unproductive in your knowledge of our Lord Jesus Christ. ⁹ But whoever does not have them is short-sighted and blind, forgetting that they have been cleansed from their past sins.

WE NOW MOVE into 2 Peter, and we can apply the practical tools for godly living in chapter 1 to our lives as well. Second Peter 1:3 teaches, "His divine power has given us everything we need for a godly life through our knowledge of him who called us by his own glory and goodness." Stop and think about that sentence. God *"has given* us everything we need for a godly life." What do you need to live a godly life and to become a godly wife? Patience? Strength? Courage? He's already given it to you. I picture a storehouse of treasures waiting for us to go and get what we need. And He has given us the key to this storehouse, "through our knowledge of him." The more we know about God and who He is, the more we will understand what He has given us. Do you desire more knowledge of our Lord?

And He has given these by calling us "by his own glory and goodness." The *NIV Study Bible* notes say: "'glory' expresses the excellence of His being—His attributes and essence; 'goodness' depicts excellence expressed in deeds—virtue in action. God uses both to bring about our salvation." He has called us because of His excellence; the excellence of who He is, and the excellence in what He does. It's not our effort but His own. Stop and praise Him as you let that sink in.

As 2 Peter 1 says, God has given you all you need for a godly life. Do you see godliness operating in your life? Through His glory and goodness, we have His very great and precious promises. What promises can you think of that meet your need today? He has given these promises so that through them we may participate in His divine nature and escape the corruption that is caused by our evil desires. Do you want to escape corruption and participate in His nature? Tell the Lord you want to take Him up on His promise.

Second Peter 1:5 says, "for this very reason, make every effort." What reason? When we see what God has done for us, giving us everything we need and the promises that allow us to participate in the divine nature and escape corruption, we have good reason to make the effort. "For this very reason, applying your diligence ... in [exercising] your faith to, develop moral excellence"—goodness—"and in moral excellence, knowledge [insight, understanding]" (AMP). Peter is telling us to make the effort to add to faith (your trust in Christ) goodness. Goodness is like God's moral virtue; it is excellence in your actions. This is virtue in action. Moral excellence speaks of integrity. How can you add integrity to your life today?

We should support our faith with goodness. It is up to you to make the effort to support the faith you have with goodness, knowledge, and the rest. Could you imagine your Christian life without any of these qualities? These are what keep your faith from being ineffective and unproductive. *Ineffective* is the translation of the Greek word *argous*, implying lazy or dead (same word in James 2:20 or Titus 1:12). It's worth memorizing the seven qualities that are added to faith in this passage and applying them to your life. If you can memorize the seven dwarfs, you can memorize seven evidences of effective faith.

The Amplified Version adds clarity by stating, "so that by them"—God's promises—"you may escape from the immoral freedom that is in the world because of disreputable desire, and become sharers of the divine nature" (verse 4). Perhaps moral excellence is the opposite of immoral freedom. Ask the Lord to show you where each is working in your life.

APPLICATION

"His divine power has given us everything we need for a godly life." What do you need?

How are you growing in knowledge of Him so that you can realize this truth? Ask God to give you the desire to grow in knowledge of God.

Write a prayer telling the Lord about your desire to participate in the divine nature and escape the corruption caused by evil desires. Include the evil desires that tempt you frequently and the aspects of the divine nature that will offset them. As you sign your name, make this a commitment to Him.

Write out 2 Peter 1:5–7, and begin today to memorize these qualities.

What would it look like to have these characteristics of effective faith operating in your life?

What would need to change?

Think specifically of this verse in light of marriage. Make every effort to add to your faith (that your marriage will be restored and that he will come to Christ), goodness—moral virtue. Does that put a new spin on your thinking?

What does moral virtue in your marriage look like? Perhaps to clean up your negativity or suspicion of him; do good to him.

#2 GROWING IN KNOWLEDGE AND LIVING IT OUT

2 Peter 1:3–9:

3 His divine power has given us everything we need for a godly life through our knowledge of him who called us by his own glory and goodness. 4 Through these he has given us his very great and precious promises, so that through them you may participate in the divine nature, having escaped the corruption in the world caused by evil desires.

5 For this very reason, make every effort to add to your faith goodness; and to goodness, knowledge; 6 and to knowledge, self-control; and to self-control, perseverance; and to perseverance, godliness; 7 and to godliness, mutual affection; and to mutual affection, love. 8 For if you possess these qualities in increasing measure, they will keep you from being ineffective and unproductive in your knowledge of our Lord Jesus Christ. 9 But whoever does not have them is short-sighted and blind, forgetting that they have been cleansed from their past sins.

WE CONTINUE TO explore the seven qualities that support our faith, listed in 2 Peter 1. Verse 5 tells us, "Add to your faith goodness; and to goodness, knowledge." Knowledge implies growing in your understanding of God. Peter talks about knowledge of God often, and this is a goal worth pursuing. Sometimes we can get so caught up in our struggles that we focus on them and stick to parts of the Bible that help us deal with the struggles or make us feel better. True growth in your faith will come as you passionately pursue God and feed your desire to get to know Him better. This is the best way to combat the false beliefs you hold about God and about yourself. What are you doing to grow in your knowledge of Christ? What would you like to be doing?

And to knowledge, add self-control. Why do you think these two are paired together? Perhaps it's not enough to grow your intellect; as we read in James 1:22, "Do not merely listen to the word, and so deceive yourselves. Do what it says." We need to put what we have learned into action. So what does that have to do with self-control? As we learn of God and His ways, we need self-control to continue to act on what we have learned, even when it's hard. Self-control and self-discipline are important in your life and marriage. I have found this is especially true when you are married to someone who has little or no self-control. Regardless of what your husband does, you need to be self-controlled and to submit to Christ's authority in your life. When you act rightly with self-control, you will honour your gospel witness.

One example from my experience is spending money; my husband is really good at that. So when I wanted something, I would hint to him and wait until it was his idea and then I could blame him. I took full advantage of that, and it was really humbling when God showed me what I was doing. I had to apologize to my husband for using him in that way.

Are there any ways you use your husband to justify your lack of self-control? Do you take more time trying to think up ways to control him rather than control yourself? Ask the Lord to reveal the things you need to change in your own life so that you can add self-control to your faith, goodness, and knowledge. We'll finish the seven qualities in the next study.

APPLICATION

Look back over the last few years of your life. Have you grown in your knowledge of Christ? Praise God for the ways you have grown. Often, we don't even realize how we have grown and changed until we stop and look back.

Ask yourself these questions:
What can I do to continue to grow in my knowledge of Christ?

Are there ways I use my husband's lack of self-control to my own advantage?

Do I think up ways to control him rather than controlling myself?

Ask the Lord to reveal the things you need to change in your life. Make an action plan to implement those changes. In one week, check on your progress.

#3 CONTINUE ADDING TO YOUR FAITH

2 Peter 1:3–9:

3 His divine power has given us everything we need for a godly life through our knowledge of him who called us by his own glory and goodness. 4 Through these he has given us his very great and precious promises, so that through them you may participate in the divine nature, having escaped the corruption in the world caused by evil desires.

5 For this very reason, make every effort to add to your faith goodness; and to goodness, knowledge; 6 and to knowledge, self-control; and to self-control, perseverance; and to perseverance, godliness; 7 and to godliness, mutual affection; and to mutual affection, love. 8 For if you possess these qualities in increasing measure, they will keep you from being ineffective and unproductive in your knowledge of our Lord Jesus Christ. 9 But whoever does not have them is short-sighted and blind, forgetting that they have been cleansed from their past sins.

LET'S CONTINUE TO reflect on the list of qualities we are to add to our faith. After self-control is perseverance. Perseverance is that stick-to-it attitude in your marriage, faith, goodness, and self-control. Continue to hope, and don't give up. Push through even in hard times. Stick-to-it-iveness is rare in our society. Challenge yourself to persevere in ways you have not before. Is your first instinct to run away? To hide or to soothe your sorrows with shopping or eating or something else? It's shocking what we run to. Ask the Lord to reveal what it is, and turn away from it! Tell Him you want to grow in your perseverance, and ask Him to show you some practical steps to put in place. Change your focus away from your own weakness and toward the Lord and His strength.

Galatians 6:7–10 provides insight on perseverance through the example of sowing and reaping. If you persevere in doing good, you'll reap a harvest. Don't give up. Perseverance will help you have an effective faith.

Add to perseverance, godliness. A godly perspective is one that puts God first in every area of life, which shapes how you think and act. God governs your attitude toward everything. *Lord, teach me to be godly in my attitudes.*

I was mulling over this perseverance and godliness pairing as I hiked this morning. Over the summer, the narrower paths in our forest often get overgrown with weeds so tall that I can't see my way forward. After a couple of nights of frost and a few snowfalls, these weeds have died and are bending low over the path. Every fall, I take the time to step on them or push them back to clear the way.

It occurred to me today that my life without godliness in action is like a beautiful trail overgrown by those weeds. It takes a lot of effort to get them out of the way so I can walk again, but as I persevere, I can see how much progress I have already made, and I know that the end is coming. I have cleared this path not only for myself, but for those who follow. My life's progression toward godliness and perseverance is like that. Would other people say you are godly? If not, what do you need to change? If they would say you are godly, is it true? What would your husband say? What does the Lord say?

The next two qualities to add are mutual affection and love. Funny that love is at the end; I would have thought this would be first. But for true love that can only come from the Holy Spirit to be evident in our lives, perhaps we need to develop all of the others first. Mutual affection is a kind and tender attitude between believers, whereas love is self-sacrificial. I guess you aren't going to lay down your life for another if you don't have affection for them first. Which are you better at—mutual affection or love? Ask the Lord to make and remake you where you need it. Ask Him to fill you with His love for others, especially your husband.

As for the connection between mutual affection and love, really, there is no love where there is no affection first. The saying, "Jesus said I have to love him, but it doesn't mean I have to like him," must be stricken from your thoughts. That's poison. It is impossible to love someone as Christ does if you don't have affection for them as well.

APPLICATION

Challenge yourself to persevere in ways you have not before. It's amazing what we run to when we don't like what is happening to us. Ask the Lord to reveal what it is, and turn away from it. Tell Him you want to grow in your perseverance and put some practical steps in place. Change your focus from your own weakness and to the Lord and His strength.

Galatians 6:7–10 is about sowing and reaping. Read this passage, and write out a parallel to your life:

> 7 Do not be deceived: God cannot be mocked. A man reaps what he sows. 8 Whoever sows to please their flesh, from the flesh will reap destruction; whoever sows to please the Spirit, from the Spirit will reap eternal life. 9 Let us not become weary in doing good, for at the proper time we will reap a harvest if we do not give up. 10 Therefore, as we have opportunity, let us do good to all people, especially to those who belong to the family of believers.

If you persevere in doing good, you'll reap a harvest. What good can you do, and what would the harvest be? Don't give up.

Would other people say you are godly? If not, what do you need to change? If they would say you are godly, is it true?

Are you better at warm affection (brotherly kindness) or self-sacrifice (love) in your marriage? Ask the Lord to remake you.

#4 EVERYTHING YOU NEED

2 Peter 1:3–9:

³ His divine power has given us everything we need for a godly life through our knowledge of him who called us by his own glory and goodness. ⁴ Through these he has given us his very great and precious promises, so that through them you may participate in the divine nature, having escaped the corruption in the world caused by evil desires.

⁵ For this very reason, make every effort to add to your faith goodness; and to goodness, knowledge; ⁶ and to knowledge, self-control; and to self-control, perseverance; and to perseverance, godliness; ⁷ and to godliness, mutual affection; and to mutual affection, love. ⁸ For if you possess these qualities in increasing measure, they will keep you from being ineffective and unproductive in your knowledge of our Lord Jesus Christ. ⁹ But whoever does not have them is short-sighted and blind, forgetting that they have been cleansed from their past sins.

HAVE YOU EVER had a time in your life when you felt you were being ineffective and unproductive in your knowledge of the Lord? I am a person who does not like to be ineffective or unproductive in anything. As I look back, I can see times when I was not living as a godly person, especially in my marriage. During these times, my selfish nature reared up, and I found myself becoming increasingly angry at my husband. I was irritable and antagonistic toward him. None of the seven qualities we have looked at in 2 Peter were increasing in my life; in fact, they were probably decreasing. That's why I think it is so important to give time and thought to what God is asking of us and how to implement that into our lives and marriages.

It helps me to remember what we have already talked about: The Lord has called *you*, by His own glory and goodness. Not only did He call *you*, but He has already given *you* everything *you* need to live this life in a godly way. Also, by His own glory and goodness He has already given *you* His promises, and through those *you* can participate in the divine nature—His nature—rather than participate in the corruption which is in the world, which you would very easily slide into because of your own evil desires (this is your not-divine nature).

Let's carry this thought a bit further. If the Lord has already given you everything you need, why have you not availed yourself of it? Ask the Lord to open you to receive. If you haven't, is it because you have chosen not to? He says "everything" you need for life and godliness. All the promises. Supplied by Him. You need to take this wonderful truth and now build your character according to the qualities, so you can be productive and effective.

Since this is what God has called you to and you have chosen it, you must now make every effort to cultivate these qualities in your life: goodness, knowledge, self-control, perseverance, godliness, mutual affection, and love. Peter tells us that continuing to grow and increase these will keep your knowledge of Him from being ineffective and unproductive. During those times when I let myself slide into ungodly attitudes toward my husband, it did seem as though I was nearsighted (American NIV) and blind, as Peter says. I did forget I had been cleansed of my sinful habits, thoughts, and attitudes, and I slid right back into them.

I have always struggled with the meaning of being nearsighted and blind. How can anyone be both at once? *Short-sighted* is the term the Amplified Version also uses. The NIV Study Bible notes suggest "an alternate meaning for 'nearsighted', namely 'to shut the eyes.'" Psalm 36:2 gives us some insight: "In their blind conceit they cannot see how wicked they really are" (NLT). We can be blinded to truth because we have closed our eyes to it, or short-sighted because we choose not to see or because evil desires blind us. Does any of that describe you? Ask the Lord to examine your heart.

I am so thankful that when we fall, He is right there to pick us up when we turn to Him. His promises are still available, He has still called us, and He still loves us more than we can fathom. When we turn toward Him, He is right there with open arms. Allow yourself to fall into Him.

APPLICATION

If the Lord has already given you everything you need, why have you not availed yourself of it? Ask the Lord to open you to receive.

We all need to grow in our self-awareness, and to do so, we must ask the Holy Spirit to regularly search our hearts and expose what should not be there. Where are you nearsighted? Where are you blind?

The Valley of Vision has a prayer titled Self-Knowledge that includes the lines: "not laying my pipe too short of the fountain" and "no one desires to commend his own dunghill."[17] How might you be laying your pipe too short of the fountain of God's abundant grace and promises? In what ways might you be trying to commend your own dunghill?

How has God been stirring your heart to respond to Him?

---

17. *The Valley of Vision*, 69.

#5 OPPOSITION AND DISCOURAGEMENT

2 Peter 1:5–9:

⁵ For this very reason, make every effort to add to your faith goodness; and to goodness, knowledge; ⁶ and to knowledge, self-control; and to self-control, perseverance; and to perseverance, godliness; ⁷ and to godliness, mutual affection; and to mutual affection, love. ⁸ For if you possess these qualities in increasing measure, they will keep you from being ineffective and unproductive in your knowledge of our Lord Jesus Christ. ⁹ But whoever does not have them is short-sighted and blind, forgetting that they have been cleansed from their past sins.

AS I HAVE worked on this Bible study, I have experienced one of the worst times in my relationship with my husband. He is constantly angry; I cannot seem to meet his expectations no matter how hard I try. In addition, we are going through a major financial crisis right now. And last night he told me he wanted a divorce! (He hasn't said anything since about it.) It was ironic to read that six months ago I was feeling constrained, and today I feel like giving up writing. Who do I think I am, telling others how they should live?

I was thinking of all I've learned through 1 and 2 Peter, and specifically the strongholds of the moment, and thought how unproductive and ineffective I feel in this knowledge right now. Is that what it means in 2 Peter 1? I want to be productive. Why am I holding back? What is going on?

Satan benefits from my discouragement (and yours). His mission is to make us give up and walk away. My spiritual director reminded me that my husband is not in control. God is, and He holds me in His hand. Of course I'm going to experience opposition to this work; it's in Satan's best interest to stop me from sharing what God has so clearly given me. So as I walked and prayed this morning, I asked God to fill me with each of the fruits of His Spirit and empty me of the opposite. To place on the clothing of Christ found in Colossians 3 and the armour found in Ephesians 6. For each piece I put on, I had to first get rid of what was there in its place. As 2 Peter says, it's easy to forget I've been cleansed from past sins (like fear, worry, doubt, pride, self-protection) and to go crawling right back to them. I didn't realize as I was trying to figure out that phrase that it was exactly what I was doing. I have been short-sighted, for sure.

Once when I was out for a walk, as I rounded a corner, a fierce dog started barking. It bared its teeth and strained at the leash to get to me. I was not afraid, however, because the owner was holding on tightly. I realized God was showing me a picture of my situation; that I may hear the growl and see the threat of the enemy, but I know who holds the leash. I finished my walk with a great sense of inner peace and strength. God had met me, and I felt prepared. We are still working through many things, but God opened my husband's heart to talk to me truthfully for the first time in many months. I leave it all in the Lord's hands.

APPLICATION

Are you participating by your actions in what God is doing in your marriage?

Is something keeping you ineffective and unproductive in your marriage? Can you identify what it is? Is it fear, doubt, discouragement, or something else? Ask the Lord to lead you into truth.

Ask the Holy Spirit to remove the "bad fruit" in your life and fill you with His fruit. Go through each of the nine fruits of the Spirit found in Galatians 5:22–23: "love, joy, peace, forbearance, kindness, goodness, faithfulness, gentleness and self-control. Against such things there is no law."

Ask God what you need to confess for each fruit. For example, the first fruit of the Spirit, found in Galatians 5:22, is love. How are you unloving? Confess this to the Lord, and ask Him to fill you with His love.

Next, do the same with the "clothing" described in Colossians 3:12: "Therefore, as God's chosen people, holy and dearly loved, clothe yourselves with compassion, kindness, humility, gentleness and patience." What do you need to take off to put on the clothing of Christ?

Finally, put on the armour of God found in Ephesians 6:13–17:

> Therefore put on the full armour of God, so that when the day of evil comes, you may be able to stand your ground, and after you have done everything, to stand. Stand firm then, with the belt of truth buckled around your waist, with the breastplate of righteousness in place, and with your feet fitted with the readiness that comes from the gospel of peace. In addition to all this, take up the shield of faith, with which you can extinguish all the flaming arrows of the evil one. Take the helmet of salvation and the sword of the Spirit, which is the word of God.

What belt do you need to take off in order to put on the belt of truth? Pray through this list as well.
And go forth in peace.

#6 DESIRING TRANSFORMATION

2 Peter 1:10–11:
[10] Therefore, my brothers and sisters, make every effort to confirm your calling and election. For if you do these things, you will never stumble, [11] and you will receive a rich welcome into the eternal kingdom of our Lord and Savior Jesus Christ.

WHAT KIND OF face do you have? I recently heard a story about President Roosevelt that described him as having a "yes" face. It stuck with me. I have a naturally "no" face.

When I was a young teen I read this saying, "At sixteen you have the face God gave you; at sixty you have the face you deserve." In my sixtieth year, I found I had cultivated a face that was miserable, with a permanent scowl and a big GO AWAY sign on my forehead. I know I have those looks down pat.

But I desire transformation, and I know you do as well. It's what's inside that shows on my face; that speaks of whether or not Jesus is in residence. I'll never forget reading, "If you have Jesus in your heart, notify your face!" I believe He is softening my face because more people seem to be approaching me lately in a way that didn't happen before. I know I want to live my life as Jesus did, in the kingdom. Impartial. Loving. Willing to throw off convention and be criticized. Doing only what the Father says. Is that your desire also? Lately my jaw has been clenched all the time, and I have to examine what I'm worrying over. Fear creeps back in so easily. I have not been as diligent. What about you?

"Therefore, my sisters, make every effort to confirm your calling and election." That means you have to confirm them (your calling and election) with your actions. Just like your face, time will tell. I've been pleading, "Lord, I need Your help!"

I want to never fall, as it says in 2 Peter 1:10. Put another way, "Therefore, believers, be all the more diligent to make certain about His calling and choosing you [be sure that your behavior reflects and confirms your relationship with God]; for by doing these things [actively developing these moral virtues (outlined above)], you will never stumble [in your spiritual growth and will live a life that leads others away from sin]" (AMP). How I long to live a life that leads others, especially my husband, away from sin!

As our study draws to a close, take a timely reminder from 1 Peter 5 to be alert, vigilant, and not to get complacent, which can be a huge problem as time goes on and things don't seem to be changing for the better. As it says in 2 Peter 3, those wonderful promises in verses 8 and 9, God isn't slow in keeping His promises; rather, He is patient, long-suffering. He doesn't want your husband to perish any more than you do. Second Peter 3:15 reminds us that "our Lord's patience means salvation." In the meantime, what you do is so important. As Peter tells us in verse 14, "since you're looking forward to this"—the Lord's coming—"make every effort to be found spotless, blameless and at peace with him." A worthy goal. The Amplified adds, "in peace [that is, inwardly calm with a sense of spiritual well-being and confidence, having lived a life of obedience to Him]."

Guard your heart against the onslaught of messages that our culture throws at us, and be wary of well-meaning people who tell you what you want to hear. There will be people who insist you should get out of your situation because "God wants you to be happy." Watch out that you don't fall from steadfastness of mind and waver in faith.

A precious promise comes from Ezekiel 36:25–27. "I will sprinkle clean water on you, and you will be clean; I will cleanse you from all your impurities and from all your idols. I will give you a new heart and put a new spirit in you; I will remove from you your heart of stone and give you a heart of flesh. And I will put my Spirit in you and move you to follow my decrees and be careful to keep my laws." Lord, take my heart of stone, and give me a heart of flesh. A new heart for my husband, my marriage. One that feels (and gets hurt).

APPLICATION

What kind of face do you have, a yes face or a no face? Try to be conscious of this over the next week; catch yourself in the mirror without changing your expression; notice if people don't approach you as much when you're brooding over something.

What kind of face would you like to have? If you could put a sign on your face for others to see, what would you want it to say? Ask God to change your heart.

What can you do to make your *calling* and *election* sure? What do those two words mean? Can you write in a sentence what your calling and your election are?

How will you make every effort to be found spotless, blameless, and at peace with God?

What messages do you have to be on guard against?

Which people come to mind who fill your head with ideas that are contrary to God's will?

Be on your guard. What can you do to make sure you don't succumb to that kind of influence?

#7 THE MOST EXCELLENT WAY

1 Corinthians 13:4–8a:
⁴ Love is patient, love is kind. It does not envy, it does not boast, it is not proud. ⁵ It does not dishonour others, it is not self-seeking, it is not easily angered, it keeps no record of wrongs. ⁶ Love does not delight in evil but rejoices with the truth. ⁷ It always protects, always trusts, always hopes, always perseveres.

⁸ Love never fails.

ALTHOUGH OUR STUDY in 1 and 2 Peter is done, there is one more passage that I want to leave you with because it is certainly "the most excellent way" (1 Corinthians 12:31). I'm referring of course to 1 Corinthians 13. Why don't you take a few moments to read through it? We are going to concentrate on verses 4–7. The characteristics of love are all found in Jesus; and He is the model for the perfect, unconditional love we want to develop toward others and specifically our husbands.

My mentor, Sue, once told me that she was taking one characteristic of love every week and working on implementing that one into her life. She studied other Scriptures where the word appeared and came up with a definition. I'd love for you to try that over the next few weeks as a conclusion to our study.

Some will need more attention than others. For example, when I read, "Love keeps no record of wrongs," I wince. This is definitely an area of my life that needs constant attention because I keep slipping back into old habits. The Amplified Version says "it does not take into account a wrong endured." So that way, it sounds as if I am not to judge in the future based on wrongs in the past. As Paul tells us in Philippians 3:13–14, "Forgetting what is behind, and straining towards what is ahead, I press on." This is a goal in my marriage, because I can't "press on" without that kind of forgetting. If my love truly does not take into account a wrong endured, then those things that I have endured can't be my filter for what I do now or how I anticipate what will happen and my motivation behind my actions toward him. I must change my expectations.

Remember: You have to serve this person for the rest of your life, no matter what his response is. So as you work through these characteristics of love, be honest with yourself. Think through each word for all its possible meanings. God calls us to live a life of 1 Corinthians 13 love; our goal is to implement all of these things that love is or is not. He is waiting for you to make the decision of your will, and in aligning your will with His, you will change in His power.

APPLICATION

First Corinthians 13:4–8a states: "Love is patient, love is kind. It does not envy, it does not boast, it is not proud. It does not dishonor others, it is not self-seeking, it is not easily angered, it keeps no record of wrongs. Love does not delight in evil but rejoices with the truth. It always protects, always trusts, always hopes, always perseveres. Love never fails." For each definition of love in this passage, work through these questions:

What ways am I strong in this characteristic?

What ways am I weak?

What ways do I need to get rid of unloving tendencies? (For example, what ways am I unkind?)

What verse can I find to remind myself daily this week?

What one(s) will be more difficult for you? Perhaps you can spend a longer time on those. Remember, He who began a good work in you will carry it on to completion (Philippians 1:6).

In conclusion, what is God's grace specifically for you that you have discovered through our study? How do you draw encouragement from that?

Second Corinthians 4:16–18 states: "Therefore we do not lose heart. Though outwardly we are wasting away, yet inwardly we are being renewed day by day. For our light and momentary troubles are achieving for us an eternal glory that far outweighs them all. So we fix our eyes not on what is seen, but on what is unseen, since what is seen is temporary, but what is unseen is eternal."

PRAYER

Lord, as my sister now commits herself to You, I ask that You wrap Your loving arms around her and hold her steady. Renew her strength Lord, as You have promised, as she waits on You. Show her glimpses of what You're doing in her husband's life and in her marriage so that she will persevere and not give up. God of hope, bring her a light. Bring her joy. Bring her peace. Amen.